It's Only A Shadow

by Nancy Hadley, Ed. D.

It's Only A Shadow
ISBN: 978-0-9833377-9-9
Copyright © 2015 by Nancy Hadley
Interior design and formatting by Grant Hill
Art design by Sarah Stratton

Published by Garden Publishing Company
10403 US Highway 87 North
Sterling City, Texas 76951

This book or parts of this book may not be reproduced in any form, stored in a retrieval system, or transmitted in any form by any means - mechanical, electronic, photocopying, recording, or otherwise - without prior written permission by the author, except as provided by the United States of America copyright law.

Printed in the United States of America.

Garden Publishing Company

The King James Version of the Bible. © (KJV)
The New King James Version of the Bible, © (NKJV)
The American Standard Version of the Bible, © (ASV)
The New American Standard Version of the Bible, © (NASV)
The New Living Translation of the Bible, © (NLT)
The Holy Bible, New International Version® (NIV®)

All quotations from NIV unless otherwise noted.
Strong's Bible Concordance.

DEDICATION

This book is dedicated to Jesus Christ.

ACKNOWLEDGEMENTS

This book is written in collaboration with Brandy Helton and Robin Reynolds. It is largely based on their personal experiences. I would not have recognized the spiritual realm, nor could I have written about it without their insight and discernment. Their voices deliver powerful testimonies. Thank you both for being my mentors and my dear friends.

I also want to thank Kevin McSpadden for his perceptive editing of this book. Kevin, you provide a valuable sounding board as well as clarifying revisions. You are a talented editor, and I am grateful to you.

In addition, I want to thank Grant Hill for his creative touch to both the formatting and to the cover design. Grant, you are gifted in ways I greatly admire, and I appreciate the opportunity to work with you. Thank you!

TABLE OF CONTENTS

Foreward   *ix*

Preface

Introduction   15

Chapter One – The Day the Axe Fell   27

Chapter Two – The Deception   61

Chapter Three – The Eyes of Fire   123

Chapter Four – Prophetic Warrior   159

Epilogue   191

Appendix   201

FOREWORD

After discussing a dream I had, Nancy, the author of this book told me that the person in my dream was the person to whom she was writing *It's Only a Shadow*. When she told me that, I could feel Holy Spirit confirming it. After reading the book, I am convinced of the truth of it.

In this dream I was in a conversation with someone. I don't know who I was talking to, but I do know that this person was a believer. This person loved the Lord and had a heart to serve Him. However, I could tell that this person felt like I was too far out there with what I believe regarding healing, deliverance, and miracles. In this conversation about Jesus and who He is, this person mentioned that Jesus was the sacrificial Lamb of God and that without the shedding of blood there is no remission of sins. I told him that I couldn't agree more and at that point something really began to stir in me. Holy Spirit spoke through me and out of my mouth came something so amazing, something I really believe but had never seen in quite this way before.

I said, "You're right! Without the shedding of blood there is no remission of sins. In the Old Testament an innocent lamb or other animal had to be slaughtered as a sacrifice for sin, and the sacrifice had to take place over and over and over. At an appointed time, Jesus arrived and became the sacrificial Lamb once and for all. It's a new and better covenant."

The other person replied, "It is a new and better covenant because now we live forever with Him and we don't have to slaughter animals every year."

I said, "Yes, but that's not all. There's more." I felt a push back from the other person when I said that there was more, and that seemed to fan the flame in my spirit. That's when Holy Spirit released these words through me.

"That Old Testament animal was sacrificed quickly. His throat was probably cut and he bled out. That's not what happened to my Jesus. I read nothing about that lamb being beaten for days and bruised inside and out to the point of being unrecognizable. I read nothing about it being spit upon. I read nothing about it having its wool plucked out by the handfuls. That lamb was not blindfolded and tortured. I read nothing about its flesh being torn and shredded into strips before it died. I read nothing about it carrying a heavy cross on its raw flesh up a steep hill. I see nowhere in the Word where thorns were pressed into the lamb's skull. I read nothing about it thirsting and being given vinegar to drink. I read nothing about spikes being driven through its extremities.

Nowhere in scripture do I read about a lamb hanging on a cross for hours until its legs could no longer carry the weight of its body and it suffocated. The Old Testament sacrifice was for the remission of sins. The beautiful Lamb of God laid down His life for everything. That's the difference between the old covenant and the new covenant. Those bruises, wounds, and thorns were for our peace, healing, deliverance, and to destroy the curse."

The Word of God will always confirm to us that we are hearing His truth. All that the Spirit spoke through me in the dream can be found in Isaiah 53. I'm adding italics and parenthesis around the words from the original language according to the Strong's Bible Concordance.

"He is despised (*regarded with contempt, despicable, worthless*) and rejected (*left, alone, forsaken*) by men, A Man of sorrows (*pain, mentally and physically*) and acquainted with grief (*sickness*). And we hid, as it were, our faces from Him; He was despised, and we did not esteem Him. Surely He has borne (*taken, carried, endured*) our grief (*sickness*) And carried (*bore, dragged*) our sorrows (*pain, mentally and physically*); Yet we esteemed (*thought, made a judgment*) Him stricken, Smitten (*hit, beaten, slain, killed*) by God, and afflicted (*put down, low, downcast*). But He was wounded (*profaned, defiled, polluted*) for our transgressions (*rebellion*), He was bruised (*crushed, shattered, broken*) for our iniquities (*perversity, depravity, guilt*); The chastisement (*discipline, correction*) for our peace (*completeness, soundness-including physical, welfare, safety, health, prosperity, contentment, quiet, tranquility*) was upon Him, And by His stripes (*bruises, wounds, blows*) we are healed (*means HEALED!!*). All we like sheep have gone astray; We have turned, every one, to his own way; And the Lord has laid on Him the iniquity of us all."

In the dream, I continued to speak to the

other person, "Nowhere in scripture is it recorded that the innocent lamb did all that. Jesus took more than our sins. The Bible is very specific about what He did. Yes, the blood of lambs was shed for the remission of sins, but He suffered pain so we wouldn't have to. That lamb didn't. Jesus was punished for our peace. That lamb wasn't. Jesus was rejected and despised so we could be accepted and adored. That lamb wasn't. Jesus was crushed for our iniquity. The lamb was slaughtered, not crushed. Jesus was ripped to shreds for our healing. That lamb wasn't. So you see, you can't tell me there isn't more.

If the Father had chosen for Jesus to die for the sole purpose of us being forgiven and getting to go to Heaven, that would have been enough, but He chose to give us so much more. To believe that all Jesus did was die for our sins so that we could eventually go to heaven totally disregards the rest of what He endured. It is almost like saying that He had to do more than the animal did to get the same results. That's just not true. If the Father intended His perfect sacrifice to be just for the remission of sins, Jesus could have been merely beheaded like John the Baptist, and the shedding of blood would have sufficed."

Consider for a moment the Lord's Supper, Communion. What are the two things mentioned? We are instructed to remember both the *body* and the blood. Jesus was very specific in His teaching and said 'as often as you do this, do it in remembrance of Me'. The fact that Jesus Himself emphasized not only the redeeming power of His blood but also what He accomplished in His body demonstrates that He intended for us to receive and live in much more than forgiveness alone. We must realize the value of the full sacrifice the Lord Jesus made on our behalf. Yes, it guaranteed the forgiveness of sin and eternal life with Him. We as believers have treasured that, but there's more that hasn't been valued nearly enough. It is the part that many put on the shelf.

Isaiah's prophesy of the coming One was fulfilled completely in Jesus. As He walked on the earth, He lived out a Kingdom lifestyle in the flesh, healing all who were oppressed by the devil, whether that be the sick, the demon-possessed, the poor, the hurting, the lonely, or the rejected. He came to seek and to save (sozo) that which was lost. Not only that, but in some of His final Words to us, His disciples, Jesus told us to do the work that He did. We are commissioned to heal the sick, raise the dead, cleanse the lepers, and cast out demons just like He did. The words 'saved', 'save', and 'salvation' are used many times in the Word of God. In fact, it is the summation of the whole Bible - the Father providing a way to bring His family home.

According to Strong's Bible Concordance, save (sozo) means *to save, keep safe and sound; to rescue from danger or destruction; to save a suffering one; one suffering from disease, to make well, heal, and restore to health; to save from the evils which obstruct the reception of the Messianic deliverance.* Soteria (salvation) means *deliverance, preservation, safety, deliverance from the molestation of the enemy, and future salvation.*

Jesus' life gave us a beautiful picture of the word sozo. When you compare the life of Jesus to this word 'save', it is a true picture, isn't it? Just as it was prophesied, Jesus lived out the full gift of salvation while He walked the earth. Finally, His passionate desire for all to live as He did was demonstrated in His crucifixion. Some of His last words to the disciples (known as the Great Commission) were a command to continue all of what Jesus showed us. That command has not ended. It is the Kingdom of Heaven, the Gospel of the Kingdom, and the Good News.

So the dream I had was really about considering something more to the incredible sacrifice that Jesus made than what has been commonly accepted, more than remission of sin. He was beaten, stripped, rejected, despised, and crushed so that we could live a victorious life in peace, wholeness, prosperity, health, and freedom from bondage in His precious name. He showed us how to destroy the works of the devil and establish the Kingdom. He gave us a Commission to heal the sick, raise the dead, cleanse the lepers, and cast out demons just like He did. He even said we would do greater works in John 14:12 (KJV),

> "Verily, verily, I say unto you, he that believeth on me, the works that I do shall he do also; and greater works than these shall he do; because I go unto the Father."

That requires us to function and even to battle in a spiritual realm just like Jesus did. That's "the more."

It's Only a Shadow presents accounts from real people who are battling in the spiritual realm. They are normal, everyday people. I join Nancy in the hope that it stirs those who love Jesus and are committed to Him in a lifetime of service to search out "the more."

—— Danetta Ferguson

PREFACE

"Is not life more than meets the eye? Is there not more to life than what we see? Is there not more to life than what meets the eye?" These are the questions Misty Edwards poses at the end of her performance of the song, "Only A Shadow", recorded from a live prophetic worship concert. Misty battled cancer at the early age of 19 and then again with a reoccurrence six years later, so her captivating lyrics authentically and eloquently delve deeply into the topic of life after death. In a reference to the valley of the shadow of death from Psalm 23, the chorus victoriously decrees

"Though I walk through the valley,
it's only a shadow; it's only a shadow!
Though my body will perish,
it's only a shadow; it's only a shadow!"

It's Only A Shadow

Later in the performance of the song, they triumphantly proclaim,

"He's (referring to Jesus) alive,

now I'm alive and I will never die."

The song celebrates the truth that although the physical body dies, there is a spiritual part of us that doesn't die. Death isn't an end; it's only a shadow.

Many believe in the "spirit" or "soul," an unseen part of a human being that exists now in tandem with the physical body and does not die when the physical body dies. Rather this spiritual part goes into a realm that is invisible for now but manifests in the afterlife. So many of us wholeheartedly believe in and rely on the spirit realm in death. We agree that death really isn't the end of existence as it appears; it is a shadow in which lies a hidden reality.

What intrigues me about Misty's song, what has become the heart of my experience, and what is the topic of exploration for this book, is the combination of the two notions that death is a shadow and there is more to life than what I see. Both point to a mystery of something going on in an unseen realm.

Many questions come to mind when thinking about these two notions together. Concerning shadows, a shadow is defined as a dark image cast on the ground from something blocking the light. If I am looking at a shadow, I am not really looking at the source that makes the shadow. Shadows of me look different depending on the angle of the light behind me, so I am missing something if I draw conclusions about myself based on looking at my shadows. That makes me wonder, if death is a shadow do I encounter other shadows in life? What is lurking in that unseen realm in or behind the shadows?

Regarding the notion that there is more to life than what I see, I am reminded that there are many imperceptible things that actually exist even though I go about my day unaware of their presence. For example, there are many frequencies my ears do not hear. It takes a radio receiver to tune into and amplify specific channels for me to hear what is ever present in the air around me. Just because I do not have my radio on, it does not mean the hundreds of channels being broadcast wirelessly are not there. I am just not aware of the different kinds of transmissions that are moving about me. What if there is a spiritual realm just as near and present as the radio signals in the atmosphere? What am I missing in my day-to-day life if I totally ignore the spiritual realm? I believe my spirit exists and will carry on after I die, but what is it doing while I am alive? Can I tune into that realm with my spiritual sense?

Because of what I have personally experienced, I do believe there is something going on in an unseen realm. I not only believe in it, I have personally encountered it. I hope by sharing some real experiences with this realm in *It's Only a Shadow* that those who have sensed "there is more" will explore their own beliefs about an unseen reality. It is my hope that many will not only wake up to the reality of the spiritual realm but will also understand that there are very real battles happening in the shadows so they must arm themselves for the fight and commit to a lifestyle that recognizes "the more."

The four experiences in the spiritual realm I share here are a combination of my own experiences along with accounts from two associates. The first story is a vivid description of hell as an imminent destination from the astute perspective of someone previously involved in witchcraft but whom Jesus rescued from the fire. The second is a riveting account of the deception in the church that keeps believers in Jesus Christ and church goers in the dark about spiritual warfare. The third is a vibrant portrayal of tangible encounters with the ONE who delivers us from hell and the deception surrounding us. The last is a thundering depiction of the reoccurring spiritual battleground that warriors face as they awaken to "the more."

As I stepped into encounters with the unseen realm, I wondered why there was so little information about it in my very traditional church experiences. After all, I grew up believing in Holy Spirit and an invisible God who lives in an unobserved realm that I will inhabit with my unseen spirit one day. In fact, I am totally relying on the spirit realm in anticipation of my death and am framing my whole life around it now, looking forward to a spiritual, not a physical, eternal existence. I know I live in an experienced-based society that relies heavily on evidence that you can see, touch, and feel to validate what is real, and unseen forces are often discounted in everyday life.

However after encountering the spiritual realm for myself, I decided that I should explore it in the "here and now" instead of waiting until death overtakes me to embrace it. I felt ill-equipped to deal with it and reasoned that I might be missing something by not delving into it now.

Many Christians would argue that the spiritual realm is a dangerous place for one to probe. However we are bombarded by vibrant depictions of an unseen spiritual realm in the movies and television. Is that safe? Crowds flock to partake in the mystical and seductive romance between vampires and humans or the enchanted adventures of wizards and witches, all under the guise of entertainment. Mediums who communicate in the paranormal between the earthly world and a world of spirits are not only portrayed on television, but are becoming commonly accepted in society as well.

Although Christians may not go so far as to consult mediums, they think watching a movie or a program on TV seems harmless. Our own children are targeted with magic and sorcery in animated films. Should I be concerned with that? Who could criticize Disney's popular depictions of monsters, magic, and fairy-tales, all of which are based in unseen reality? We tend to categorize such entertainment as meaningless fun, but is it possible such things have very real consequences?

Why is talk about Holy Spirit hushed in that same prolific entertainment industry, much less in some of our own everyday and/or religious conversations? If I am totally reliant on my spirit at the end of my life, why do I feel ill-equipped to deal with subjects that relate to it now? If I evaluate content honestly, there is a lopsided treatment of the spiritual realm in entertainment and even religious circles. On the one hand, it is defined as a dangerous realm for serious study, and on the other hand, participation with dark powers under the guise of entertainment is commonly accepted. After my own encounters with deception, I am not surprised by that.

In my quest for information, I looked in the bible at what Jesus said first when He started His ministry. There must be something significant about the first recorded words of His ministry. After He emerges from the desert where He was tempted by the devil, Jesus refers to an unseen kingdom, the kingdom of heaven, being near.

"Repent, for the kingdom of heaven is near" (Matthew 4:17).

Repent means to change the way you think, so He was talking about changing the way we think about an unseen reality. He says that the kingdom of heaven is not far but near. Does He mean near in time or in space or both? Invisible reality is also acknowledged in passages such as 2 Corinthians 4:18,

> "So we fix our eyes not on what is seen, but on what is unseen. For what is seen is temporary, but what is unseen is eternal."

Jesus responded to people and situations as if He saw something others could not see. For example, in the middle of the crowds gathered at Capernaum in Mark 2, some men lowered a paralytic through the roof to see Jesus because they could not get to Him any other way. Jesus' first words to the man they lowered did not concern his obvious crippled condition. Jesus said, "Son, your sins are forgiven" (Mark 2:5). Jesus later healed the man by telling him to get up and go home, but He first dealt with the man's spiritual condition.

After a similar healing in John 5, Jesus talked about only doing what He saw His father doing,

> "I tell you the truth, the Son can do nothing by himself; he can do only what he sees his Father doing, because whatever the Father does the

Son also does" (John 5:19).

Jesus was talking about things that were very apparent to Him but not in plain sight to the people around Him. In Mark 5, Jesus has a conversation with the spirits collectively called "Legion" who inhabited and spoke through a man who lived in the tombs. Jesus cast the spirits out and into the pigs. He was both conversing with and defeating demons in a *spiritual* realm.

Similarly, the bible confirms the existence of evil forces in the unseen realm in many other places such as Ephesians 6:12,

> "For our struggle is not against flesh and blood, but against the rulers, against the authorities, against the powers of this dark world and against the spiritual forces of evil in the heavenly realms."

I have been intrigued with the number of references to the battles in the spiritual realm and have sought to equip myself for the battle. Throughout the bible, there are countless passages and numerous references to angels as well as other supernatural beings interacting with people and surrounding God in His dwelling place. All of these passages deal with an invisible space. How, therefore, can we learn to recognize and even function in such a realm?

As I studied and grew, I learned that Holy Spirit is my true guide to the unseen realm, and I learned how to discern His voice from other voices that might try to influence me. Testing the spirits is essential – it is the first and most important step. First John 4:1-3 (NKJV) says,

> "Beloved, do not believe every spirit, but test the spirits, whether they are of God; because many false prophets have gone out into the world. By this you know the Spirit of God: Every spirit that confesses that Jesus Christ has come in the flesh is of God, and every spirit that does not confess that Jesus Christ has come in the flesh is not of God. And this is the spirit of the Antichrist, which you have heard was coming, and is now already in the world."

So there are spirits in the supernatural domain interacting with us to sway our behaviors, which means we must be diligent only to listen to the Holy Spirit. Only He can equip the believer to thrive in the spiritual world.

Instead of an exhaustive study of what the bible says about the unseen realm, of which there are many excellent ones already written, Holy Spirit directed me to share a bit of my own journey within the spiritual dimension along with some truths I have discovered along the way. Once I started this journey, I found many individuals and groups already on the same path who are much further along than I am in discovering and describing this realm and how it affects both day-to-day living and planning for eternity. I am seeking to add my experiences to the body of works already out there. I hope my accounts confirm what others have already found.

I urge those who are beginning this exploration to take the time to consider the vivid descriptions I present in the formulation of their opinions.

Preface

These accounts may seem far-fetched, much like the portrayals of the supernatural in the movies. However, be assured they are real and recorded by experienced individuals who have carefully considered biblical foundations and equipped themselves for spiritual warfare.

It's Only a Shadow attempts to provide an introduction to a biblical view of the spirit realm, heightens awareness of spiritual encounters, honors Holy Spirit, glorifies Jesus, the King of Kings, and opens up the possibility to the reader that what we see is only a shadow!

INTRODUCTION

The suggestion that there is something greater behind what we see is as old as Plato's 380 BC writing, the *Allegory of the Cave*. Although I am not a disciple of Plato nor am I aligned with all of his works, this piece graphically illustrates perceptions of the unseen dimension that existed long before Jesus came to earth with His descriptions of it. In Plato's allegory, or parable, he describes a scenario in which prisoners are held captive for their entire lives in a cave, facing a blank wall, looking at shadows projected on the wall from various objects passing in front of a fire from behind. Chains keep the captives in place from birth, and they grow up unaware of what lies a few feet behind them and who is orchestrating the shadows.

In Plato's metaphor, the adult detainees spend their time analyzing both the projected images and the echoing sounds from the wall. Some of them become good at predicting the order of the shadows and are promoted within their society, which defines the nature of the world from shadows on the wall.

What the captives take to be real is in fact a delusion. Plato's allegory depicts an uninformed humanity trapped in an illusion of truth and completely unaware that the widely accepted perspective they all share is the result of the chains that limit their perspective and the powers arranging the shadows.

Plato takes the analogy even further to explore what such a prisoner would do if he were released from the chains and shown the fire behind them or even dragged into the light outside the cave. The prisoner would of course be blinded by the light at first, but once his eyes adjusted to the light, would he trust what he saw or would he be drawn to return to the comfort of the cave? How would he now view what he once believed? If he were held in great esteem within his society because of his ability to predict the shadows, what would he do when he came to understand true reality outside the cave? Would he give up his position to accept what he was shown?

How would he handle living color when he was used to dark shadows? Furthermore, if he returned to the cave, could he convince the other prisoners of the new reality? How would the society within the cave treat him when he returned? Would they accept him and the wisdom he brought or would they reject him along with the truth he conveyed?

As Holy Spirit awakens believers to the spiritual dimension, many find themselves facing the same tough questions as Plato's enlightened prisoner. Believe me, I was as surprised as anyone when I found myself trying to answer these questions about a world I had vividly encountered.

I first caught a glimpse of something more than meets the eye while standing in my kitchen. I relate it to Plato's *Allegory of the Cave* because I saw for myself a reality outside what my senses could perceive. In my mind's eye, it felt like I was suddenly at a movie theater in front of a huge screen watching a

It's Only A Shadow

panoramic scene of a vast land with rolling hills and cities. There were people moving about normally, but they had shadows of themselves that resembled the form of the person as a shadow does. However, the shadows were not dark but translucent, so it was like I was seeing double.

The "doubles" moved separately from their matching persons, and some of the "doubles" were close in distance to their respective persons whereas some were not. The people and their doubles were connected by a thick, translucent cord of light. In addition, the people were unaware of the existence of the watchful presence, "the cloud of witnesses" that were watching from above. However, the doubles seemed to be in contact with the witnesses.

The scene reminded me of the movies, *The Matrix* and *The Truman Show*, because in those movies for the most part, many of the characters go about their business unaware of the existence of the watchful presence of the people behind the scenes. In the movies, the characters believe their perception is reality when in fact, reality is something very different. From my vantage point in the vision, I could see the reality behind the scenes, and the reality was that the people were totally unaware of the presence of both the doubles and the witnesses. To me it seemed like I was observing the spiritual realm and how it operated. The doubles appeared to be spirits of the ones to whom they were connected, and the witnesses were ones who had gone on to be in eternity.

I felt like I was at a cosmic a sporting event where the spirits, both the doubles and the witnesses, were watching the players, or people, on the playing field. The spirits watched closely the events taking place and cheered at various intervals. However, while the atmosphere so closely resembled a sporting event, the picture itself was a normal, everyday activity.

As I studied the scene, I noticed that the people were unaware of the spirit realm or how their actions affected their doubles. The doubles, however, were keenly aware of their corresponding "player" and were shadowing them, closely watching their movements. I saw the doubles turn to one another and "high five" when their corresponding people did something that made a difference in the spiritual realm. The celebration moments corresponded with breakthrough moments in the action when the spirits got a message through to the people. Each connection from spirit to person was like a goal scored.

As I continued to watch, I perceived that the spirit, or double, was bound or restricted in some way to the actions of his/her player; therefore, it was imperative for the two dimensions to be in contact with one another. However, I could tell that it was difficult for the spirit to make contact with the player. Once again, the prevailing feeling was like a sporting context, so this instance was like a moment in a sporting event when the coaches on the sideline were exuberantly reacting to the success of the players. The chief aspect of the celebration was that the spiritual realm was breaking through and impacting

Introduction

the play.

I was amazed at what I saw in my mind's eye, and it took some time to unpack the significance it. Since that time I have been acutely aware of the spiritual realm around me. I chose to give credibility to what I saw. That was definitely an important choice in my journey and one that opened my "spiritual eyes." Some would say that I have an active imagination and would discount it as anything useful in exploring the mystery of the spirit realm. I say that I experienced it and it has helped me understand the very real, unseen world.

Once my spiritual eyes were opened and I became aware of the way unseen spiritual forces worked in my daily life, I saw how God was moving in our area in the physical world along with the supernatural forces that were opposing this move. For example, during my morning walks which I dedicated to purposefully listen to the Lord, I perceived spiritual battles with my spiritual eyes. The battlefield looked like one from the movie, *Braveheart*, but the warriors were people I knew. One day I would see a group of us all dressed in armor gathering around an early morning campfire, planning a strategy for battle. The next morning I saw the same group, only it was missing one person. Once again, I paid attention to what I was seeing with my spiritual eyes and took notice instead of brushing it off.

At the same time in the natural, I was involved in a team of people God was assembling who were studying spiritual warfare together and pursuing what we felt God was leading us to do. The members of the team were prophetic people who were highly aware of spiritual warfare and involved in God's work in our city.

The group was drawn together because of an awareness of their prophetic purposes and gifts, and they had a vision of the spiritual dimension of everyday life. These were the same people at the campfire and sure enough, the one that was missing from the campfire was the one who, for one reason or another, was not participating with the group as much. I saw it first "in the spirit" and then it occurred "for real." Not every daily occurrence was highlighted on my morning walks, but enough of them were to cause me to take notice. I began apprising the team of my morning perceptions.

One day Holy Spirit told Brandy, the leader of the team, to tell the story of the spiritual warfare that both she and the team had experienced in real life. Communicate it, He said, like a story told in movie format. She began to disclose it during our gatherings on Sunday nights, and as she did, the instances to be included would be revealed. Sure enough, as Brandy talked about the battles we had really experienced, the layout of the story was uncovered.

It's Only a Shadow records the first four incidents Holy Spirit highlighted. There are three "voices" or perspectives from the team in the accounts: Brandy's, Robin's, and mine. We included only the details that Holy Spirit allowed, fashioned it into a narrative from a perspective that recognizes spiritual warfare, and changed the names of others to protect their identities. The events that are recorded are actual events from our perspective, and the point of the book is to reveal the reality of the spiritual realm in everyday life along with strategies we learned through "on the job training" in spiritual warfare. It identifies spiritual concepts working behind the scenes in real life situations and spotlights unseen forces that may be casting the shadows on the walls.

As the stories are told, remember that all is laid bare in the spiritual realm, so the descriptions are quite graphic. In telling the actual details of these stories, we face the same issues within our society, which discounts a spiritual perspective, that Plato's returning cave captives might expect to experience.

Most people ignore the vivid spiritual struggles we sense on the heavenly battlefront. Many deny the forces that drive those who are unaware they are being driven. What proof can we present to an unbelieving society that the spiritual dimension really exists? How do we handle the possible rejection of the insights we bring from the spiritual perspective?

Introduction

Using Plato's terms, we are presenting a story from "outside the cave," and we are willing to give up our positions in society "within the cave" in order to share it. It is my hope that after reading these accounts readers will begin to question their own beliefs concerning the unseen realm to determine the truth in this mystery. I pray that you recognize the light that shines beyond the cave of your perceptions and that you find the courage to see what that light shows you.

Chapter One

The Day the Axe Fell

A few years ago, God placed Brandy in a spirit filled church where she served the Lord by making disciples, equipping them through His word and the Spirit to see them mature in Christ Jesus. The pastor of the church recognized Brandy's gifting and insight, and after seeing first hand her prophetic gift and her passion to see the captives set free, he chose to release her to minister deliverance to the congregation. "Deliverance" means she ministered healing to the brokenhearted and helped those held captive in bondage to be set free.

God's word reveals kingdom principles for the believer to follow that will bring freedom or deliverance. These basic yet powerful tenets include repentance from willful sin, forgiveness of others and oneself, destroying curses, and renouncing lies believers have agreed with about themselves and others. Demonic spirits will leave under the authority Jesus gave those who call Him Lord and Master. Deliverance assumes that even Christians can be plagued by the devil, and it cancels the ill effects intended to neutralize Christians in spiritual warfare. When deliverance begins in a church, when the light is unveiled and people begin to understand that freedom from bondage in this world is a part of the salvation package along with eternal life upon physical death, the strongmen from the darkness that pull the strings on the people in the congregation appear front and center to challenge the unveiling of this truth.

Although Jesus calls all to Himself, giving an opportunity for all to come to repentance and freedom, no matter the level of darkness operating within, most are unaware of the battle in the unseen realm as they respond to this call. Once the anointing, or "the burden removing, yoke destroying, power of God," is revealed through His servants, the enemy often launches a full scale attack and releases strategies to hinder or eliminate the one carrying that anointing.

With the blessing of her pastor and the anointing Jesus had given her, Brandy had worked with many to see them delivered. One day the pastor brought Robin to Brandy, believing for her freedom. Since Robin was innocently drawn into witchcraft during her childhood, she was in deep need of God's love and healing. As Brandy pursued her in love at the Lord's direction, Robin became very special to Brandy, and Brandy began to walk with her personally to disciple her. In the process of bringing freedom to Robin, the demon spirits would from time to time oppose Brandy, the anointing, and the word of God through Robin.

However, it was never in Robin's heart to oppose Brandy. When heaven invades earth and light confronts the darkness, there is retaliation in the spirit realm from the powers of darkness. Ephesians 6:12 (NKJV) states,

> "For we do not wrestle against flesh and blood, but against principalities, against powers, against the rulers of darkness of this age, against spiritual hosts of wickedness in the heavenly places."

The individual being delivered can be deceived and unaware of the powers that operate through them.

In His goodness and wisdom, the Lord works with individuals differently based on their heart and needs, and therefore, freedom is like pealing the layers off an onion. It can happen in stages over time. Due to the increasing warfare over Robin's deliverance, the Lord led Brandy to fast all communications with Robin for a time so that Jesus could reveal Himself to Robin and strengthen Brandy in the process. The following event occurred the first Sunday after the fast ended.

It was a normal Sunday service in Brandy's

church. The sanctuary was a semi-circle with pie shaped sections for the pews facing the platform at the front. The congregation gathered as usual without a hint of what was happening in the eternal realm at that very moment. Brandy, on the other hand, came to the service with a heightened spiritual awareness. She had recently received a word of knowledge, a message from Holy Spirit, "The Book of Jude is in your church."

The book of Jude is a small book in the Bible, just before Revelation, and it is a reminder of what is false and how things can creep into a church to oppose the church. It's a warning. If that wasn't sobering enough, Brandy had a vivid, open-eyed vision that shook her. She literally saw a person completely on fire, burning. The person was running out of the fire. Verse 23 of Jude raced in her mind with the message, "Snatch others from the fire and save them."

During the worship part of this day's service, Holy Spirit spoke to Brandy again, saying, "Get up and go check on Robin." So Brandy got up from her place in the front of the congregation and exited the sanctuary through one of the side sets of double doors that separates the sanctuary from the front of the church. Robin was there in the foyer, bending over to peer in through the crack in the center set of double doors. Brandy walked up behind her, feeling the full weight of anointing and intensely aware of the spiritual dimension.

Before the service began that morning, Robin had noticed four people enter the sanctuary, and when they did, she immediately felt uncomfortable. During the worship part of the service, Robin was enjoying one of the songs, "Thank You for the Cross", when she felt a dark demonic presence come over her from behind. The feeling was so overwhelming during the song that all she could think about was that she needed to keep an eye on the four people who had entered the church. Robin stated:

"I was very uneasy at these four coming

in, but I was also uneasy about some others. Two weeks prior when Brandy wasn't there, two women whom no one had ever seen before came in the sanctuary. They manifested, loudly calling out in some weird, demonic language at one point during the service. Everyone tried to ignore it or say they just weren't right mentally. There had been some weeks of these people showing up randomly, unknown to so many. Someone was singing the song "Thank You for the Cross." I loved that song and would always feel the Holy Spirit's presence so powerfully during it that I could always just let go in worship. But that morning, I felt the two realms collide during the song. I did feel the Holy Spirit's presence at first, but then I sensed this huge power of darkness. Because we were singing of the cross, I knew that it had to be opposition from the people who walked in previously. I felt like nobody was aware of what was going on in the demonic or spiritual realm. It had been five weeks since I spoke to Brandy. During this fast from talking there was an incredible personal and spiritual battle. I was sensing, knowing, seeing, and experiencing the forces of darkness and the kingdom of light in a battle that I had never encountered before."

So Robin, stirred by the clash in the spiritual realm, had also left the service during worship and was keeping watch over these four people. Robin continued:

"Due to my background I knew how the enemy could use people to oppose or release curses upon those within the church. As I was standing there bent over looking through the crack of the door, I felt God's presence behind me."

Because the Lord had prompted Brandy to check on Robin, as soon as she walked up Brandy knew something was wrong. Robin turned to find Brandy with her arms crossed gazing at her. Due to the conflict between darkness and light in the spirit, Robin was startled so she gasped for words with, "Brandy, what are you doing?" Brandy threw back, "What are *you* doing?"

Robin nervously diverted the confrontation with, "I'm just watching these people who came in." By now, Brandy was operating in the spirit, and it was as if she had left the physical locale and was now functioning in the spiritual dimension. Robin related:

> "I immediately sensed the authority and presence of God in Brandy. I also remember that inside I was trembling because I felt like something huge was fixing to come down, but I had no idea what. I experienced so much fear due to the opposition of powers I

was feeling."

Although Robin had been through some deliverance and had experienced partial freedom, the ruling, controlling spirits over her were still able to operate through her. In the full anointing, Brandy burst into tongues, her spiritual language, as she addressed the opposition coming through Robin in the spirit realm. Instantly, Robin shot back with a demonic tongue. By this time, Robin knew the difference between the demonic tongue that she spoke and tongues from Holy Spirit. The clash was intuitively hostile between the two powers of light and darkness.

Inside, Robin became instinctively horrified because even though she did not know what she was saying, she knew she was speaking in a false tongue that was opposing Brandy. She knew there was a force among them that was incredibly strong. Robin had no control to stop what she was doing and she knew she was hurling threats. In the midst of the heated exchange, much to her horror, Robin began to laugh at Brandy in a demonic, mocking way. She remembered:

> "This was absolutely the worst feeling. I really felt as if I was split in two. It felt like I was two different people, but as it is in the demonic, the demonic often splits our senses. I know that my senses were split or divided. Here was the demonic coming through me, I was so aware of it, and I couldn't make it stop. It was as if I could hear and feel the presence of the demonic coming out of my physical body, yet I could see it in the natural and with the Presence right there. It was almost as if half of me was in the demonic and half of me was seeing from the anointing (not that I was in the anointing but the anointing Presence was right there touching me)."

The only way Robin could figure out how to

make this whole exchange stop was to leave, so she ran outside to try to compose herself.

Grounded back in the physical realm but still spinning with the force of the events, Robin found herself outside the building, repenting for the behavior she was unable to stop. She did everything she could to say she was sorry for all that had transpired. Robin recalled:

> "I ended up on the ground beside the wall crying out to God to make the demonic stop and to come save me. I repented to Him over and over, and I kept telling Jesus I was so sorry for what I just did to Brandy. I asked Him to forgive me more than once. I was so terrified. I asked Him to just destroy all of the darkness, get it out of me, and keep it away from me. I told God that I didn't understand what was going on. I cried out that I felt like I was losing my mind, and no one understood or cared. I told Him how scared

I was at seeing all of this demonic and not knowing why this was all happening and how it was working through me. I was pretty much begging Him to come do something. My heart was still beating incredibly fast, and I didn't know what to do, so I just chose to come back inside."

Once Robin had somewhat composed herself, she re-entered the building and peeked through the doors. There was a break in the singing and everyone was quiet. She frantically searched for a safe place to go and spotted her husband, one of the ministers of the church, standing in the back of the sanctuary on the opposite side of the room. So she went to stand by him. Robin recollected:

"When I first went and stood beside my husband, I remember just trying to 'act' normal, but I felt sick. I was still reeling from what had just taken place outside in the foyer as well as my time outside with the Lord. I can still remember standing against the wall with my husband beside me. Some announcements were made. I think even a short video was shown, and I began to feel something coming in my heart. It felt like brokenness or when you feel as if you need to cry. It felt and looked real hazy, kind of like the feeling you get when you are about to pass out."

At that point, the congregation began another song with everyone looking toward the stage area. All of a sudden, the scene morphed into a vision, and Robin was engulfed in the spiritual realm, but this time it was a full blown, open-eyed vision. She sensed that she was standing in a doorway, even though she didn't see one, and she instinctively knew she was in an entrance into something but was afraid to move. She spotted the four individuals she had been watching, and she felt an intense heat. Unbelievably, one of them ripped off part of his forearm, grabbing chunks of flesh off of his own arm, and ate it! As she looked at their bodies, they appeared horribly decayed with bulging eyes. In Robin's words:

> "The doorway (that I didn't' really see) was the first thing I sensed, but really that one guy eating chunks of his own flesh to stay 'alive' was the first real thing I saw. I couldn't move from where I was. It was like I knew not to take a step into this place."

Robin began to process what she beheld, and as she looked around, she could still see impressions of the sanctuary, but now not all of the people were sitting in the pews that were previously in view. It reminded her of the "Left Behind Series" where people were present one minute and were instantly snatched away the next. There were definite vacant spots throughout the sanctuary where previously there were people. Robin continued:

"I also remember at first wondering why there were people from the sanctuary missing, yet some were in this place. The eyes were bulging out of everyone's heads, and everyone's veins were massively popped out. People's flesh that they were taking off and eating looked just like 2nd and 3rd degree burn patients. Some of their flesh was just hanging and so red and oozing, and then other parts of it looked whitish-black like a charcoal grill. The people seemed so unaware and acted as if it was normal to be in this place."

The next thing Robin knew, she was hearing incredibly awful sounds. There were nonstop, horrendous groans and demonic screams getting louder and louder. She looked down and the ground was a grotesque sight, oozing like lava in a bloody mixture. The sounds became even louder and Robin began to shake, feeling she was right on the precipice of something monumental. Now she knew she actually was looking into Hell, seeing a part of eternal damnation before her very eyes. To her horror, she looked down to find herself pulling the flesh off her own arms. She stated:

> "I did pull the flesh off of my own arm, but I never ate it because as soon as I pulled it off, I was horrified at the way I touched it and it came off. At that very moment the sounds intensified."

Little did Robin know that in the very next moment the Lord would reveal both Himself and the truth as He came to destroy the work of the devil and the witchcraft that had ruled Robin her whole life. Horrendous trauma and witchcraft had led to the formation of multiple identities which kept her emotionally and spiritually enslaved at various ages. These traumas caused her to stay trapped at the age these events occurred.

As the grotesque sounds became even louder, all of a sudden, a giant axe appeared over Robin's head. It was massive, to the point that she only saw the head of it. With a thundering whoosh that overtook the sounds she was already hearing, the axe fell over her, slicing through her body from head to toe. The axe cut through all of the multiple identities that had plagued her in her tumultuous past, severing them from her for good. With that decisive blow, she was out of hell and out of the vision.

Instantly she felt a massive grief come up and out of her. She trembled and shook because she knew she was had literally been right at the entrance of Hell. She concluded:

> "The final thing that I saw was the cross and the blood of Jesus. I remembered the song that was being sung that morning that stirred all of this to happen was 'Thank You for the Cross.'"

It was the most vivid reality Robin could ever have experienced. She knew the veil between the natural and spiritual had dropped, and she was shown that she was at the entrance of Hell and was about to take a step into it. Nervously, she looked to see if her husband had seen any of it.

Trembling, Robin thought about what had just taken place with Brandy. The passage in Mathew 7:22-23 (NKJV) flashed in her mind,

> "Many will say to Me in that day, 'Lord, Lord, have we not prophesied in Your name, cast out demons in Your name, and done many wonders in Your name?' And then I will declare to them, 'I never knew you; depart from Me, you who practice lawlessness.'"

Robin realized that the people she saw sitting in the pews were either already in Hell or they were facing the same decision she was facing. Because of the revelation of the cross and the axe that came down, she was faced with a choice of life or death - true repentance or total destruction. She could no longer deny the truth of what had happened to her in childhood, and God was giving her the choice to come out of the captivity of witchcraft and the terror therein. He was offering freedom from the powers that had been operating through her without her knowledge. God offers repentance through Jesus Christ to all who are enslaved in sin and bondage.

Robin immediately looked for Brandy, who was standing against the wall opposite in the back of the sanctuary, still praying in tongues. Weeping because of the trauma of what she had just experienced, she made her way over to Brandy. It was truly life changing for Robin. Immediately she wanted to tell Brandy about her rescue, repent to her, and ask her for forgiveness for the demonic tongues. With fire in her eyes, Brandy refused to touch Robin, but directed her to a small bridal room to continue the exchange. Unable to stand, Robin fell on her knees repeating one thing over and over, "I am sorry, I am sorry, I am sorry."

Brandy was unaware of Robin's vivid encounter but highly aware of the spiritual battle in which she had just been engaged. Something operating through Robin must have been aroused during Robin's surveillance of the four people, and it was the heated exchange of tongues that caused Brandy's response. Consumed with the Spirit of Truth Brandy boldly addressed Robin, saying, "Choose you this day who you will serve." The message was clear and the line was drawn in the sand. Brandy would no longer entertain the powers that had been operating in and through Robin the last three months. The Holy Spirit had revealed the same message to both Brandy and Robin and it was clear to Brandy not to talk to Robin any more in that moment until the Lord brought wisdom. Brandy let Robin know that she would be in contact with her later. Brandy related:

> "After church I was still on fire and yet deeply grieved and broken over Robin. I prayed and asked God how He wanted me

to walk this out. I was encouraged by a dear friend to let Robin go for a season and to allow the Lord to finish His work without me helping her. My husband encouraged me to ask Robin to fast for the next three days and allow the Lord to speak to us all. I did release her to Jesus. This was one of the hardest things I had done yet. I had labored with Jesus to see people freed, but I was not the ONE who would ultimately free them. So, I called Robin later that evening and told her of my decision and gave her the specific instructions I had been given by the Lord."

Robin remembered the instructions:

"Brandy would contact me after those three days if the Lord allowed her to. She told me to read Jude. She actually told me twice, and I knew she was trying to tell me something without actually saying it. I knew her well enough to know that she couldn't say it all to me because the Lord wouldn't let her, but I knew that I needed to search it out.

That night after Brandy finished talking to me on the phone, I came back inside my house, sat down, and read Jude twice. Right away, I knew what the Lord was showing me, and I realized instantly that I had been plucked out of the fire. On that Sunday, what also happened is that for nearly three months I had felt overtaken by the enemy and all of his plans and schemes. I had hit a point of believing that nothing in me was good or of God anymore. I had no hope left of escaping the enemy. In a matter of minutes, the Lord's wrath, judgment, and His love for me destroyed - in a few minutes - what the enemy had taken three months to build up. God allowed me to see how big He really was compared to the enemy because the enemy is so good at making himself look bigger than God. I knew the Lord rescued and saved me, but I felt, understood, and saw the seriousness of how close it was."

Robin fasted the next three days and did not communicate with anyone, but focused on the truth that Jesus was the author and finisher of her faith. What she had seen with her eyes and what she had actually experienced that day was so real to her that she was totally willing and ready to say yes to the repentance that was offered to her.

Nevertheless, Robin was grappling with the sin or iniquity that was in her family line. She had previously denied it and therefore had not accepted responsibility for it. Occultism and witchcraft were ingrained in her family line before she was born. Once Robin was born, the iniquity that is passed from generation to generation came to her. Robin had no choice concerning the horrific things done to and through her, but even though she had no choice, the sin remained. During this time, however, she was granted godly sorrow for generational sin, and this sorrow reached deep within her spirit, surpassing human understanding. She clung to 2 Corinthians 7:10,

> "Godly sorrow brings repentance that leads to salvation and leaves no regret, but worldly sorrow brings death."

This Godly sorrow produced life within her. Describing the three days in Robin's words:

> "Monday was my day that I spent in repentance, praying and just seeking revelation of it all. I began to understand the iniquity. I began to see how the enemy's plans had unfolded as well as the time frames he had laid out. I spent the day awed that I let Satan do what I let him do to me and how he used me. I still felt sickened and held onto a Godly sorrow at what had unfolded the past three months and over the weekend.
>
> Tuesday was my day of 'iniquities,' where

I just spent all morning in total repentance and brokenness before the Lord. I had already spent five weeks repenting, confessing, etc., but this was different. This was a deep, true repentance that leads to life and that leads to no regrets, whereas the other times of repentance I often repented because I felt sorry and bad for sinning, but also that I'd been caught. It's the kindness of the Lord that leads us to repentance. So this day I repented, renounced, broke, confessed, forgave, and released. I went back to the church and had an amazing time with the Lord in prayer and worship."

At the end of the second day, the heaviness broke over Robin, and she felt the release from her decision to embrace the sorrow and accept the repentance she was offered. She spent the rest of the day rejoicing in worship and encountering the Lord in the spirit realm. Whereas she had experienced

Hell only days before, with the same reality she encountered the Lord. She describes:

> "I was at the point where I was asking the Lord to just come take all of the shame, guilt, and condemnation because it was more than I could bear, as well as the fear. With each exchange healing would come and I felt incredible love from Him. At one point I was actually standing before the Lord telling the accuser to get behind me. A white turban was placed on my head and a new robe was placed around me."

For two days Robin was immersed in sorrow and repentance. She realized her participation and accepted the opportunity to repent and receive the robe of righteousness provided by her Lord. Robin describes the last day of fasting:

> "Wednesday was my day of new begin-

nings and continual praise and worship in Him and giving Him all the glory. I drew pictures this day as they'd come in prayer. One I titled, 'A Brand Plucked by the Fire' and I used the scripture from Zechariah 3:1-7. Another picture had to do with being cleansed from curse and from multiple generations of curses. Another picture was about the Refiner's Fire and Fuller's Soap from Malachi 3, where Jesus is the fuller's soap to me as well as the refiner's fire.

During these three days, at first my emotions were of such 'shock and awe' filled with the shame, guilt, and condemnation at what had happened and what I'd been involved with. The second day, I felt like I had a fire in me. I felt angry at being used by the enemy, and I felt angry at the iniquity. By the time my three days were up, I just was so thankful to be offered repentance, for the cross and the blood of Jesus that takes my iniquities away. I was so thankful that the axe had come down to save and that I was no longer living in torment from the enemy that had been consuming me 24/7."

The light poured in and the darkness fled. Robin realized that the axe fell that day to break through all of the iniquity of her family and all of her sin. God had answered her prayer and offered her repentance. Her acceptance of the responsibility for the sin and her true repentance sealed her freedom. She saw the axe cutting through all of her multiple identities stemming from trauma. In one monumental blow, she was separated from her past. Later, in discussions with Brandy, Robin drew a clear distinction between multiple personalities and multiple identities. With her unique perspective, she described the difference:

"I've said multiple personalities, but I've also told Brandy before it was multiple identities. There's a difference at least in my experience. I remember when Brandy was sharing with me about another lady's multiple personalities, and Brandy didn't know if she needed to help her get set free by addressing each one individually. I immediately told her that she didn't need to spend time addressing each one because based on my experience with the axe, God could get them all in one cut.

From what I understand in my limited training about multiple personalities, people who suffer from multiple personalities have other people inside them, who are actually spirits with names. For example, let's say there is a woman named Sally. Inside that woman there may be a little girl named Sue, an old lady named Alice, a seductress named Carol, and a mother named 'mother.' When Sally takes on the persona of another personality, she would actually think she was that person, play the exact part of that person, and call herself by that name.

With me, it felt more like multiple identities, meaning I was always 'Robin.' I never took on a personality of another person, but my multiples were 'ages.' So in me there was Robin as a 5 year old, Robin as a 9 year old, Robin as a 6 year old, and Robin as a 13 year old. In deliverance I literally had to be healed at each age where the massive trauma happened. At each specific age, I was still trapped, and it was as if that event that happened at that age wouldn't let me grow up past that age in a specific area. We did deal with events from many of these ages, but it was as if I was still somewhat imprisoned in my mind at each of the ages. When the axe came down that day, it cut through all entrapment of the ages so that I could then begin to totally deal with it all. I could no longer live as a 5 year old or 6 year old or 10 year old in any respect. I could instead see myself at each specific age and deal with it as an adult. Even though in getting healed I would feel the pain of the little girl, I didn't 'become' the little girl anymore."

For Robin, the day the axe fell it permanently severed all sin, all iniquity, and all identities forever in one decisive blow. Through God's grace and mercy and through her acceptance of what was offered in these supernatural encounters, Robin's final freedom came. Robin was the one in the vision that Brandy saw being snatched out of the fire in the middle of the church. Robin was saved.

The Day **The *Axe* Fell**

Chapter Two

The Deception

Throughout the time Brandy ministered deliverance, she was operating under progressive revelation from Holy Spirit, who guided her step-by-step in understanding the forces at work not only in various individuals, but in the territory as well. The revelation always came just when she needed it with strategies to deal with what was manifesting at the moment. She followed John 16:13 (NKJV),

> "However, when He, the Spirit of truth has come, He will guide you into all truth; for He will not speak on His own authority, but whatever he hears he will speak; and he will tell you things to come."

Brandy literally received on-the-job training in the various degrees of spiritual warfare. At first she dealt with "ground level" deliverances in which she identified and cast out demons in normal, everyday individuals. Later she was trained at a higher level of warfare against higher powers including witchcraft against the church. Although Brandy had read books on the subject, she was thrown into intense battles as she faced the formidable forces that were assigned to keep Robin bound.

Amazingly, many of Robin's memories were totally blocked because of the programming administered to her by adult authorities throughout her childhood and the deception she was under. She was completely unaware of how the powers of evil were affecting her. Because those who are deceived are totally unaware of the deception, the deception cannot be addressed, much less removed, and therefore it remains "under the radar," undetected, and unattended. It takes the Spirit of Truth operating either directly or through another person to expose the deception in order to break the bondage.

Deception is one of the many tactics Satan uses to oppose God. The purpose of deception is to keep people from encountering God and from receiving revelation of His Word which will empower them and free them. The ultimate battle in deception is against God and His Word, but it manifests in and through people.

Robin gave a chilling description of the power of the deception over her through no choice of her own:

> "Brandy was the first person in all of my adult life who had ever taught me that spiritual warfare was a reality. Of course I knew about the basic warfare and attacks from the enemy as the church had taught me to expect those in my Christian walk. However, I'm talking about the kind of spiritual warfare that's at a much higher level. It's the kind of warfare mentioned in Ephesians 6:12 where

you do not war against flesh and blood but powers and principalities. My natural, carnal mind was like many Christians in that I didn't want to acknowledge the depth of the spiritual warfare or attacks as truth. Yet my spirit man knew exactly what Brandy was telling me. The Word of God and the power of the Holy Spirit were backing her up. As more deliverance and revelation came to me, I realized that I knew way more about spiritual warfare than most. Light was shining on darkness, and the love of Jesus was flooding my entire being. The depth of the warfare, the knowledge of the enemy, and the depth of the darkness that I had encountered my whole life was coming forth.

For about a year, we'd been praying through layers of deliverance issues that would surface. Brandy addressed me twice as a 'witch' and showed me the iniquity or sin of participating in witchcraft. The second time that

The Deception

she addressed this in me, the fear of the Lord and His truth fell upon me. I had spent some weeks before this time engaging in conversations with another person, who also had some mixture just as I did and was in the process of being set free as well. I was listening to and talking about things with this person in the natural and spiritual realm that were not of God, yet my mind was so veiled and deceived that I never ever had a thought that what I was doing was witchcraft or even demonic. Revelation had to come.

For days I would pray over what God was revealing, and I continued asking for revelation of what I didn't understand or couldn't see concerning the iniquity and its position within me. I was finally taking this whole identity of a witch, witchcraft, and occultism seriously. I knew there was a mixture in me because of how I would manifest at times both in prayer and in conversations. I was horrified at the thought that it could be true because of my hatred of all witches, warlocks, demons, freemasonry, Satanism, and occultism. Why would I want to do or be a part of something that I despised so much and wanted to get away from? That didn't even make sense.

Can a person be a witch without choosing to be one or without knowing they are one? When I was in the third grade, I went to a birthday party and spent the night. My parents did not know that the girl's mother was a practicing witch. She took us in a room, had us put our hands on a crystal ball, and told us how to become a witch. She had a black cat, a broom, her hats, and other items.

This woman had willfully made a choice to become a witch. Because of this experience I assumed that anyone who was a witch had chosen to be one. I had not chosen to be a witch as this woman did. In answering the question about choosing to be a witch, let me give some more insight from my own background.

During the time period of this testimony, I was in a fight for my life to get free from the occult and abusive past that was still being revealed to me. For three months that fight consumed me 24/7, and I felt as if I had lost my mind. No, I didn't choose to align with or participate with the occult. It was forced upon me. My alignment had already happened in the woods with my relatives when I was a little 6 year old girl, and I didn't choose it then. That alignment was broken in the natural when I was 15 and moved away from exposure to the occult through my relatives. From the time I was a young child to my teens, all positions and assignments were forced, and I was filled with fear.

Many times, I would get punished with each 'event' that would happen because I was rebellious to the demonic assignment that was in both the natural and the spiritual. Even at a very young age, I would somehow know that it wasn't right, and I was always looking for an escape route or a way to get free. In the spirit, the alignment with the occult did not break until the day I made Jesus both Lord and my Master. It was completed the day the axe came down. Due to the amount of trauma in my life, iniquity in my family line, my own sin, and being programmed, I was unaware, enslaved, deceived, and veiled to the witchcraft and my participation with it until it was revealed during the layers of deliverance.

Now back to the question that I asked earlier, can a person be a witch without choosing to be one or without knowing they are one? The answer is YES and NO! In my case, I did not willfully choose to become a witch. I was forced into it as a child. Others can enter witchcraft this way as well. However, some willfully choose this path of deception.

Remember, I had been seeking the revelation on all of this. My heart was open to the truth and I had repented of all that I knew of to repent. The most confusing part in so much of this time period was distinguishing what was truth in the natural and what was truth in the spiritual.

The fear of the Lord was all over me, and then after some time, the Truth began to come forth. The Holy Spirit gently revealed to me the answers I had been seeking. He not only allowed me to see the depth of the iniquity through my family line and the deception that was there, but also allowed me to see how it was at work in the church.

The day I got the revelation concerning how I had been participating with witchcraft, I cried all day and repented with such a Godly sorrow. I experienced horror, shame, guilt, and condemnation along with such anger at certain people in my past. I quickly prayed through these feelings and exchanged them with Jesus because I knew they were not from Him. Praise God that His love, forgiveness, mercy, and grace was poured out over me.

However there was one thing that still troubled me. Brandy had become a very special friend who had been literally laying down her life for my freedom. She freely gave me everything that she had been given and co-labored with Jesus to bring me out of regions of captivity in the spiritual realm as well as helping me deal with situations in the natural. Most of all, Brandy loved me with the love of Jesus, and it was that love that was setting me free. Why was there such a battle between us at times? Why did I find myself sometimes opposing her and opposing Jesus Christ working through her?

The *Deception*

The enemy was in full force against me and against Brandy for several reasons. When a person tries to get free or actually makes an escape both in the natural and the spiritual, the dark powers will do everything to find them, stop them, or stop the one who rescues them.

Escaping and finding freedom in the spiritual realm is often much more difficult than escape and freedom in the natural realm. Because I was breaking away and getting free, because I'd made Jesus the Lord and Master of my life, and because I was exposing truths (even though I still had some mixture), the enemy was very stirred up. I knew the enemy wanted to use me to get to Brandy. I knew she was the 'real deal' and that she had the anointing of Jesus Christ in and on her, so I knew to protect her.

Even in the midst of me being used against Brandy for the enemy as well as all of the manifestations that I had during that whole year of trying to get set free, I never wanted or tried to go back to the spiritual forces of the occult. There were many who told Brandy to give up on me and quickly get away from me because they felt I could never be able to be free due to the depth of the witchcraft, occult, Satanism, and high demonic powers that I had been subjected to and participated with in my life. I guess they didn't know the power of the Most High God and what His love will do.

If I was truly trying to align with the occult, then some events that happened would not have happened the way they did, even though I still participated with the enemy. My participation was there so 'evil happened.' I was on my way out, not in! I just hadn't made it all the way out yet. Even when the axe came down, I wasn't trying to align with darkness. I was trying to get free from those powers.

It's as if there were two parts to this deliverance process with me. One had to do with Brandy. Never in my whole life had I ever manifested as badly as I had with her during that first year. It's the weirdest feeling to be freaking out inside and not know why or what's going on (even though the demon spirits in me did) and at the same time you look into someone's eyes, such as Brandy's, and see a love that you've never seen, known, or felt before. Brandy was in this territory to answer the cry for freedom and to rescue captives with the love of Jesus. She was sent to establish a five-fold government and to set apostolic authority in this place. Jesus was in her eyes.

The other part to this was me simply wanting to be free in my spirit, soul and body because that is a promise and a benefit that I receive from making Jesus Christ my Lord and Master. He went to the cross for me to have complete freedom. I wanted to be free from my past, the occult, the abuses, the curses and assignments, and from all that was causing me bondage, fear, and torment. I was trying to get free from a spiritual realm that had become my natural. It is a realm in which no one wanted to believe or acknowledge. I escaped the occult only through the blood of Jesus, through the cross, and with Brandy being used as the vessel to do it."

Brandy had been called to a movement of God in the territory that she did not even know about and found herself operating in an all out war. Strategically, the enemy engaged her early in an intense, high-level battle with the occult in the spirit realm to see Robin freed from the witchcraft by which she was bound, relying heavily on the grace of God for every move.

Witchcraft is traditionally defined as the craft

The Deception

or trade of those who exercise supernatural powers through the aid of evil spirits. In 1 Samuel 15:23 (NKJV), the bible calls witchcraft a sin and equates it to rebellion: "rebellion is as the sin of witchcraft."

Those overtly practicing witchcraft are defiantly disobedient in their willful use of malicious powers to oppose, manipulate, and control others by a whole litany of practices including voodoo, curses, spells, hexes, vexes, and incantations. The underlying purpose is to assign demonic powers to manipulate people into doing something other than what God intended for them to do in order to oppose God and foil God's call on their lives. These witches often use intricate schemes to place curses on curses, which fall on the inexperienced warrior who dares to break the initial curse.

Although there are many areas of the world where witchcraft is openly practiced with witch doctors and voodoo priestesses, there are other areas where the exact same spirits of witchcraft are hidden and accepted under the disguise of the prevailing cultural customs or under the pervasive practices of manipulation and control. This can include passive aggressive behaviors.

Statements such as "he is so controlling" or "she manipulates with her helplessness" reveal common participation and ignorant acceptance of witchcraft. Even when one is doing what he thinks is best as opposed to what God tells him to do, this behavior is characterized in the bible as witchcraft because of the rebellion.

Saul participated with witchcraft when he willfully chose to disobey the voice of God because he "feared the people, and obeyed their voice" (I Samuel 15:1-35, ASV). It cost him. He would no longer remain as king over Israel. Disobedience to a mandate from God is rebellion, which is witchcraft.

Because of the level of the occult that had dominated Robin at such an early age, Robin had difficulty even identifying things that were normal to her as connected to witchcraft. The extraordinary level of deception kept Robin in the dark as to how she was being used in the opposition to Brandy, and it kept Brandy scrambling to understand exactly how to maneuver the mine fields deliberately placed for her.

Because "all is not fair in war," the enemy used Robin, even as she was being freed, to continue his assault on Brandy. For example, Brandy and Robin were sharing a room with two other ladies at an *Open Heavens* conference, when, to the amazement of all, demonic spirits invaded the room with a loud thud. Everyone jumped at the noise and Brandy discovered that the bible that was positioned on the desk in the room had suddenly been chunked into the trash can across the room. Later Brandy was startled to hear Robin audibly cursing Brandy in her sleep. Robin muttered a variety of things to oppose and to bring sickness and destruction on Brandy's physical body, family, finances, relationships, and even another apostle who stood by Brandy. Brandy immediately arose and wrote the curses down.

The next morning when Brandy confronted

Robin with Robin's own words from the night, Robin immediately replied without thinking, "I only do this during the night and not during the day!" This statement revealed the extent to which the whole process worked. Robin knowingly cursed Brandy in the night but had no remembrance of it during the day.

Through the deception, Robin separated what was ingrained in her nightly activities, with her reality in the day. Because she had not connected these activities, she was astonished and horrified at how she opposed Brandy when her actions were identified. Immediately, Robin responded by asking Brandy to pray for her, destroying the behavior. Every time Brandy brought light to her actions, Robin quickly and decisively repented, destroying another layer of the deception that was deeply rooted. What was perfectly clear to her outside the veil of deception was totally obscured while she was underneath the veil.

The iniquity operating in Robin was not unlike the residual lust in men that gets a free ride with "boys will be boys" or the lust for power operating in Simon the Sorcerer, who offered money to buy Holy Spirit even after he was saved. The spirits remaining in Simon wanted to buy the power because sorcery is all about the power. Peter responded by pointing to the lingering iniquity inside Simon in Acts 8:23 (NKJV), "For I see that you are poisoned by bitterness and bound by iniquity." Simon immediately repented in the next verse, "Pray to the Lord for me," as did Robin.

Brandy believed the goodness of God and the proximity to the anointing at the conference exposed this remaining but secret threat. Ephesians 5:13-14 corroborates Brandy's conclusion, "everything exposed by the light becomes visible; for it is light that makes everything visible."

Perhaps the greatest deception of all is the grossly misunderstood, catalytic power of words in the spirit realm to bless or curse. Proverbs 18:21 clearly states,

"The tongue has the power of life and death," and James 3:6 says,

> "It [the tongue] corrupts the whole person, sets the whole course of his life on fire, and is itself set on fire by hell."

God created the entire world by speaking His Word, and because man is created in God's image, man's words have the same power to stimulate action in the spiritual realm.

Both angels and demons await assignments issued by the words released by man to carry out either blessings or curses, setting in motion events that create or destroy. "Mere words" carry enormous power so the enemy begins spinning the deception early with nursery rhymes such as "Sticks and stones may break my bones, but words will never hurt me." Nothing could be farther from the truth. According to Isaiah 55:11,

> "So is my word that goes out from my mouth: It will not return to me empty, but will accomplish what I desire and achieve the purpose for

which I sent it."

Releasing God's word in a situation calls forth the spiritual resources to finish the job. Brandy was speaking the Word of God, striking terror amongst demonic forces that rose up against her, so they were determined to take her out.

Curses are the empowerment for evil and blessings are the empowerment for good. Although the bible is full of admonishments concerning words, even some believers in the Word carelessly curse their children or themselves with statements like, "You'll never amount to anything" or "I'm such a klutz," when they are in fact assigning spiritual forces that will make their declarations come true. The devious deception surrounding reckless use of words alone keeps many people bound by hidden forces hurling destruction.

Many would be appalled to discover the damage their words have caused even to their loved ones. No one argues with the uplifting power of encouragement or the insidious power of false accusations to destroy someone's character, but few recognize the truth that the corresponding spiritual powers are released and assigned. Idle words set in motion the same powers as a deliberate curse.

Intentional curses call forth demonic influences that oppose an individual but Proverbs 26:2 (NKJV) states,

> "Like a flitting sparrow, like a flying swallow,
> so a curse without a cause shall not alight."

In spiritual warfare, it is crucial to understand what is meant by "cause," or legal ground, so that the demons can be commanded to leave. If the armor is intact, fiery darts cannot penetrate, but if there is a "chink" in the armor, the weapon penetrates through the weakness.

With Robin, Brandy was cutting through Robin's entanglements to free her from the lingering influences of the witchcraft from which Robin was fleeing. Although Brandy could not prevent the enemy from attacking, she had to make sure to shut down the effects of the curses hurled her way by closing the door to any legal ground for tormentors to operate. Forgiveness and obedience call forth blessings and remove legal ground or "cause." Brandy regularly practiced both by the grace of God and to the best of her ability.

However, removing "cause" did not prevent Satan from continuing the barrage of attacks on Brandy. She was too dangerous, and in spiritual warfare, it is important to note that Satan does not play fair. Brandy poured all she had into Robin and others to see them freed, healed, and made whole. She discipled them in the word of God and was equipping them for the work of ministry.

For a brief time, before the axe came down for Robin, both Robin and others were used by the enemy to wear Brandy down. For example, one person would take a nose dive requiring much prayer with Brandy, while Robin seemed to be on level ground. Conversely when that person got better, Robin would fall, requiring intense prayer with Brandy. Brandy remembered:

"I was actually on the phone with Robin one night talking and I was addressing some darkness that had arisen within Robin, when I heard the Holy Spirit speak to me the word, 'twinning'. He showed me that Robin and another were being used in this method. I had not even seen that happening to me. I was just laboring with them because of my great love for them both!

In that same conversation, I quickly spoke to Robin of what I had just heard the Spirit speak and the demon within Robin responded with "Ha!" I was challenged by the spirit guarding the 'high position' or 'level' that Robin had held, in that she couldn't be released. With fire and boldness in the anointing, I responded to the challenge with God's word even as David did when he found himself before a giant mocking the army of God. I spoke his words to this mocker, 'Who is this uncircumcised Philistine, that he should defy the armies of the living God?' (I Samuel 17:26). David found himself before an enemy, 'a giant' that in the natural had an entire army in fear. Through David's faith in his Living God, he knew God would defeat his enemy, despite the boasting and mockery of his foe!"

Concerning this same event, Robin described:

> "Brandy was constantly praying with one of us to get us set free. It was as if several of us were twins and we were using a programming technique called 'twinning' to wear Brandy down. In other words, if one of us was weak, then the other one would be strong. We would never get set free at the same time. We'd never be strong at the same time. If one would manifest then the other wouldn't and as soon as those manifestations were over and done with, then the other one

would manifest. We kept certain pieces of information silent to protect the other one in the spirit.

During the time Brandy was helping us get free, our participation with the witchcraft was due to 'controllers,' basically a form of programming. We were both taught to self-destruct at certain times in our lives if anyone ever found out what we knew. In the natural, we both had experienced LOVE because of Brandy, and both of us knew that we'd been taught and trained to be a sacrifice. Because of the love of Jesus that came through Brandy and because of the freedom we were getting, we really didn't want anything to happen to her. Yet it didn't matter if something happened to us because of the 'twinning' and because we could turn on each other if needed. Due to the lack of understanding that we are created by God as spirit beings, many only look at witchcraft in the natural and physical, but in the spirit it's always bigger than can be imagined."

This diabolical technique wore Brandy down. Miraculously, in response to Brandy's cries, Holy Spirit revealed this "twinning" technique to Brandy. When a warrior is aware of the enemy and is equipped with a prayer strategy to take to the battle, she can effectively defeat the enemy. Again, Brandy received progressive revelation as to the prayer strategy and as James 5:16 (KJV) states,

> "The effectual fervent prayer of a righteous man availeth much."

Now she knew. She was aware of the technique so she cut the cord of twinning between Robin and her friend and destroyed the assignment. Brandy's faith was again and again increased as she received just what she needed when she needed it to apply to the fierce and deadly undercover battle.

Deception operates at various levels in different individuals, but with the same efficiency in keeping those who are seeking a higher power just out of reach of the truth. Robin's deception was carefully orchestrated throughout her childhood under a cloak of secrecy. She was totally unaware of the powers operating through her. Until the day the axe fell, spirits of witchcraft continued to operate, causing a mixture of influences, both light and dark. Through the deception secretly positioned on her, those powers were present wherever Robin was and accompanied her into the church. In Robin's own words,

> "I believe the witchcraft was already in the church. It didn't just come in because of me, though I had witchcraft in me. I believe that, in essence, several of us were used to bring it to light."

Congregating within any church gathering are people with varying degrees of understanding and participation with the spiritual realm, along with varying degrees of deception operating within those people. The church is the government of God set up to administer His goodness, bring His kingdom to earth, and save the souls of all mankind. Unlike Robin, who was totally under a shroud of deception, there can be "plants" from the enemy in the church. These people are definitely aware of the spiritual realm but have aligned with the darkness to block the pursuit of truth within the church. They deliver curses and leave, or they infiltrate to assume position within the church for the purpose of taking out the pastor, destroying the prayer structures, and causing other problems.

As Brandy progressed in her training, she would learn to battle on this strategic level of warfare, but for now, she dared not engage the enemy on her own without clear direction from her mentor, Holy Spirit. Brandy remained submitted to the authority of the local church pastor, battled witchcraft within the will of a converted believer, and awaited direction from Jesus, the Captain of the Hosts, to make any high level moves.

Even among members of the church who support what the pastor is preaching, there can be deceptions. Some may be inadvertently participating with witchcraft through the frivolous use of the tongue or through fascination with witchcraft-promoting entertainment. The powerful attraction to horror, vampires, and sorcery under the guise of harmless enjoyment is pervasive even in the church. The allure to this type of amusement is a deadly agreement with unseen, evil forces, presenting cause for those forces to enter. Those caught in this illusive trap are engaged in entertainment for sure. However, they may be as appalled as Robin was when she found out she was cursing Brandy if they could see exactly who they are entertaining and what they are allowing to influence their lives.

The pastor or leaders may even fall into rebellion when they deem the congregation not ready for a valid mandate from the Word of God. The mandate they reject could either be directed to them, or they could oppose an authorized mission from a member of the congregation, thus hindering the call on the member and causing the pastorate to ignorantly participate in witchcraft.

In all of these cases, believers have entered the Kingdom of God, they are born again spiritually, they love Jesus, and are seeking God; they simply have not been delivered and are blind to deception. Of course there are those like Robin who are in the process of and have experienced varying levels of deliverance.

Once believers step into the kingdom, Holy Spirit works to bring deliverance and to uncover all of the hidden things to remove deception. Holy Spirit continues to grant repentance through the renewing of the mind by the Word of God, and the Lord delivers, heals, prospers, and restores the believer to wholeness in body, soul, and spirit. In 1 Thessalonians 5:23-24, Paul delivers the word,

> "May God himself, the God of peace, sanctify you through and through. May your whole spirit, soul and body be kept blameless at the com-

ing of our Lord Jesus Christ. The one who calls you is faithful and he will do it."

When Holy Spirit brings an issue to light, the believer has the choice of whether or not to repent. Repentance brings freedom from the assignment associated with the sin, but if the believer does not repent, the forces that were operating through the deception still have legal ground to operate. So although saved, the believer can still be in bondage during this life. The demonic spirits do not reside within the spirit of the born again believer, but within the body and the soul of the believer in the mind, will, and emotions.

New believers have experienced a degree of change and freedom in that they have been "born again," but often times they have not changed their sin habits and have not had the demons behind these habits cast out. These filthy spirits that have gained entrance into the believers' lives because of any one of a number of open doors such as un-forgiveness, willful sin, curses, trauma, vows, and judgments.

The Deception

These converts have never had curses destroyed, and they are still in bondage, many times through deception.

Still oppressed and afflicted, some new converts may also have wounded hearts. As they are in the process of deliverance, working out their "salvation with fear and trembling" (Phil. 2:12), the demons that remain hidden within the soul and/or body still have access to them and can operate through them against others.

Nancy was one of those people who were saved but needed deliverance. She heard of Brandy through a mutual friend who had prayed with Brandy. Nancy had been in a prayer group with her friend for twelve years, so they had a solid spiritual relationship. Her friend's powerful testimony drew Nancy to contact Brandy. Though Nancy wasn't sure what exactly was drawing her, she knew she needed to check it out. Nancy and Brandy met with an instant resonance in the spirit. Brandy directed Nancy to read a book describing deliverance, *Shadow Box-*

ing by Dr. Henry Malone. After reading the book, Nancy found herself identifying with many aspects of those needing deliverance. She was ready to approach the process, yet totally unaware of the veil of deception that covered her and what would transpire in the deliverance session.

From childhood, Nancy's perceptions made her conscious of the spiritual realm. She sensed things beyond her physical reach and often had vivid dreams of that reality. Not finding answers about these perceptions within her church experience, Nancy was drawn as a small child to explore such things as Ouija boards with her best friend. She later naively dabbled in New Age and holistic medicine. Nancy had received Jesus Christ as her savior as a young child out of the fear of going to hell conjured in vacation bible school. She followed her older brother down the aisle and with the resulting baptism, felt reasonably comfortable that she would get to heaven upon her death.

Later in life, Nancy recommitted her life to

Jesus, this time not out of fear but out of choice and was subsequently re-baptized. Rising up through an academic environment until she earned a doctorate in education, she was well schooled and considered herself relatively knowledgeable and living a normal, Christian life. In Nancy's words from her journal:

> "Jesus said, 'If you hold to my teaching, you are really my disciples. Then you will know the truth, and the truth will set you free.' (John 8:31-32). I thought I knew the truth, but did I know the whole truth? I guess the evidence of knowing the truth is the degree to which you feel freedom. I felt freedom from condemnation and saved from my sins, but the truth was that I was not free from the torments of what I considered to be everyday life. I didn't know I could be free from torment!
>
> I am a respectable Christian, from a respectable family, in a respectable profession,

living a respectable life. As a matter of fact, I had long considered myself an above average spiritual person. Attending church regularly, participating for twelve years in a weekly prayer group, journaling my spiritual walk, studying religious materials, and conversing regularly with my Savior well qualified me as a practicing believer with a personal relationship with my Lord. Although I had my share of skeletons in the closet, even my torments were well within the realm of normal. Yes, pride does indeed proceed the fall, and I definitely fell."

One of Nancy's torments was a reoccurring physical ailment, so enlightened in popular culture, she did not see any danger in utilizing the benefits of holistic medicine under Dr. "G." After all, she had seen some positive results in battling this aliment through Dr. G and openly testified of the benefits of such treatments. However, she never got completely healed and subjected herself on a monthly basis to his prescribed treatments for many years. These remedies became progressively more unorthodox, but Nancy had an open mind and she trusted Dr. G's explanations. At Dr. G's recommendation, she delved into books about quantum healing and other therapeutic traditions and rationalized that she could take advantage of a variety of treatments at no cost to her own spiritual standing. She had no understanding of the power of agreement or alignment in the spiritual realm; therefore, she was blind to how her acceptance of various healing techniques opened the door to the powers behind those practices. She thought she had it under control.

Adding to the medical aspects of Nancy's justification, Dr. G was an attractive man, and he playfully complemented Nancy along with mentally stimulating her. This synergy kept Nancy reasoning that others just wouldn't understand, so she didn't talk much about the large amounts of money she was spending for the treatments or divulge the uneasiness she felt at times.

Inadvertently, Nancy kept the sketchy parts strategically hidden, so as not to come under scrutiny by anyone who would hold her accountable. As the years went by, Nancy sunk deeper into the deception, unaware of the bondage that had ensued by her open minded participation in and tolerance of the alternative medical practices of Dr. G. Nancy continued in her journal:

> "It was no stretch for me to believe that we are continuously involved in spiritual warfare and that Satan uses the desires of the flesh to neutralize and entangle believers. I knew about demons and could see the effects of demonic possession on evil people. However, I never envisioned the extent to which believing the lie had empowered the liar in my own life. I rationalized I was an upright Christian with traditional beliefs, living a good life.

The Deception

When I heard about the Spirit of Infirmity, I knew I had to learn more. My most angelic friend recounted her deliverance from perpetual headaches through her incredible journey, which started by first reading the book, *Shadow Boxing*, then praying with Brandy, who had an anointing for spiritual warfare. Her tears of joy accompanied by an unmistakable gleam in her eyes convinced me of the integrity of her story. I had been wrestling with chronic sinus and ear problems many years and the thought of freedom from the grips of those nagging irritations fueled my interest. Although my friend mentioned breaking strongholds in her life, it was the victory over this Spirit of Infirmity that intrigued me. After she placed this powerful book in my hands, I began my own extraordinary expedition."

The deliverance session that marked the

journey's beginning was not what Nancy expected. Nancy's dear friend had described her session as a peaceful one where she took deep breaths and easily expelled the unwelcomed spirits. Nancy had quite a different experience. She met with Brandy and another lady whom Brandy had taken through a few layers of deliverance.

The deliverance group met at the church where after a beginning prayer, Brandy started by having Nancy talk about her story. As Nancy talked, Brandy recognized situations in which un-forgiveness presented legal ground for spirits to operate, and she presented Nancy with the choice to forgive.

After the explanation that forgiveness was a choice, not necessarily deserved by the perpetrator, Nancy chose to forgive each time, closing the open doors to unwelcomed spiritual forces. If she had chosen not to forgive, the doors would still be opened, which would allow future intrusions from the enemy. Over the course of the session, Nancy recanted vows, broke curses, cut unhealthy soul ties, and repented of judgments that invited assignments from the enemy to invade her life. After the open doors had been closed, the scene was set for the spirits of darkness to be expelled. Nancy described the shocking events that ensued:

> "When Brandy got to casting out the spirits, I was horrified at what took place. All of a sudden I was unable to control my body. I was sitting in the chair and my shoulders began to writhe like a snake. There were swells of movement that would start in my core, twist through my torso, and exit through my head and shoulders, thrashing my head from side to side. One shoulder would rise and as it fell, the other would rise in an oscillating fashion.
>
> Each time Brandy would address the manifesting spirits, the movements would increase. To my horror, I had absolutely no control over my body. I literally felt the spir-

its hanging on to parts of my physical body as they were being pulled out of me, kicking and screaming. I was appalled at both the number of spirits and the intensity with which they held their ground.

I remember at times as Brandy was commanding the spirits to leave, my head would shake from side to side in defiance. That part really amazed me. Here I was telling spirits to leave with my voice and my head was shaking like a rebellious child saying, 'NO!' There seemed to be a fight between me and the spirits for my physical body. That was surreal.

Brandy would call forth my spirit into action and tell me to take charge with my own voice. Sometimes, I would force sounds through my gritted teeth. I kept repeating, 'It is my choice and I choose Jesus.' At one point I was begging the spirits to leave, and Brandy corrected my pleading approach, encouraging me to take the authority I had no idea I had.

Finally after what I thought was a lifetime, the spirits left, the writhing stopped, and my body became calm. Although my muscles, particularly in my shoulders and neck were aching, I regained control over my body. I literally could not believe what had just taken place.

I was nervous driving home, and when I finally got in bed, I shivered under the covers. What would I do if those spirits came back on me? Could I call Brandy in the wee hours of the morning? Brandy sent me home with a list of scriptures proclaiming who I am in Christ. I clung to them, looking for one that I could assure me that I would be okay. The verse that saved me that night was 1 John 2:27,

> 'As for you, the anointing you received from him remains in you, and you

do not need anyone to teach you. But as his anointing teaches you about all things and as that anointing is real, not counterfeit — just as it has taught you, remain in him.'

I knew what I received was the real deal. After all, those powers were forced to relinquish control of my body. I received a power that remained in me, and I did not need Brandy to fend off whatever might come back. I did not need anyone to teach me. His anointing remained in me. I successfully fought off the fear that knocked on my door and rested in the reality of that verse.

The next morning, I went into the kitchen and opened the cabinet containing all of the pills and remedies prescribed by Dr. G. Those familiar, rationalizing thoughts began flooding my mind again. Perhaps I could still use these pills at no cost to my spiritual welfare. What could it hurt? Were the spirits in the literal pills? Could I trust what had happened last night? Was it real? I had a large supply which constituted a considerable amount of money. Maybe I could use them up and just not order more. What a waste of good supplements and money!

As I pondered these things, I felt the soreness in my neck and shoulders and was overwhelmed with the vivid memories of the previous evening. Although I did not think there was anything inherently wrong with the pills themselves, I decided to take no chances. I made up my mind to take my stand. I gathered all of the pills and threw them in the trash as a gesture to show my break from dabbling in and depending on questionable sources. Before I could change my mind and lapse back under the spell I knew I was under with Dr. G, I called his office, canceled my next appointment, and told the receptionist, 'I will not be back, I have been delivered.'

In retrospect, I am grateful for the physical manifestation because without it, the deception was so strong on me that I am not sure I would have believed any such spirits were real. My academic powers of rationalization would have discounted any such experiences as a hoax. I had never conceived that such things could happen to a normal, church-going, intelligent, reserved person, much less me!

What I experienced was anything but normal. It transformed my life in a supernatural way, to the point that I see everything from a totally different perspective. My conventional resignation to life's trials has been demolished along with the strongholds I didn't even know existed. I am astonished by the freedom and resulting joyful peace I feel. Jesus tells us not to 'keep on babbling like pagans' (Matthew 6:7) but to pray to God, 'your kingdom come, your will be done on earth as it is in heaven' (Matthew 6:10). On earth as it is in heaven, now. The whole truth puts the realm of heaven in the 'here and now' and I can personally attest to it."

Nancy was delivered from many things that evening, but it was her submission to Dr. G's ideology and the powers operating through him that created a mixture not unlike the mixture operating in Robin when she came out of witchcraft. Nancy was genuinely operating on the truth she knew, but did not have a grasp of the whole truth. She had no idea of the extent of freedom Jesus had purchased on the cross. Although she could readily perceive the supernatural realm, she did not have the discrimination to distinguish between the different types of powers. Unaware of the dangers of dabbling with "energies" and naive concerning the use of the term, "higher power," Nancy blindly stepped into alignment with a false power. She bought into the deception that Christians cannot be infiltrated. That proved to be a dangerous assumption.

Although saved by Jesus Christ, Nancy submitted herself to treatments from other sources, mixing the powers that had influence on her life. The key was in the submission and it was her submission that left her vulnerable. In her pursuit of victory over infirmity, Nancy deferred to a false power operating through Dr. G. His mantras were more than harmless words spoken over Nancy, and her agreement with them opened the door and gave the beckoned spirits legal ground to stay.

Nancy never asked Dr. G what his beliefs were and better yet, did not think that his beliefs would matter. She knew he was trained in a variety of eastern medical traditions, but in her mind, she was merely utilizing the benefits of his treatments, which included some unorthodox ways to determine what was wrong along with some spiritually charged techniques and remedies. Nancy never saw putting her trust in the man for her health or accepting his treatments as coming into alignment with anything

The Deception

negative from his belief system. She never dreamed that through the years, she would be inadvertently inviting assignments against her that kept her body in torment and her finances drained.

Just as Nancy witnessed how vehemently the false spirits held on, she also beheld the glorious power that drove them out. She would see that power more clearly later, but for now, her life was forever changed by the way the demonic had manifested in her physical body and was driven out. This would not be the last time Nancy was rescued on a deliverance battleground either.

Those who are deceived are totally unaware of the deception; otherwise they would not be deceived. The power of deception is that it is not perceived. If it is not perceived, it doesn't exist to the unsuspecting person. If knowledge of the deception is blocked, the deception cannot be addressed, much less removed.

Deception flourishes when understanding is blocked. No matter how complete or how powerful the deception is, it can be removed. "It was for freedom that Christ set us free" (Galatians 5:1, NASV). Jesus, the King of Glory, the wonderful One who came to save the world and not condemn it, and who "always lives to make intercession" (Hebrews 7:25, NKJV) for us will break through the veil of deception over the one being delivered by the power of the Holy Spirit. Jesus will reveal Himself as He truly is and will reveal His love and goodness towards the precious believer seeking Him. In His light, no deception can stand.

Jesus revealed Himself to Robin as well, and it was this revelation that convinced her that she was worthy to be released. Robin describes her miraculous encounter:

> "It was an early Monday morning at church somewhere between 4:30 and 6:30. I joined Brandy, Nancy, and a few others early on Mondays to pray. Brandy had been doing this for some time as the Lord had directed her. Each of us spent our own time

with Jesus doing whatever the Holy Spirit showed us to do. Sometimes we would pray corporately and other times we would still be praying individually, but each of us could feel what the Spirit was saying and showing. We had no agenda but to do His will, encounter His Presence, worship His mighty name, and cry out for a revelation of His love as we believed for the miracles, signs and wonders. More than anything we just wanted Him!

Each Monday Brandy would bring in a cd with a playlist that she had burned for the week. Usually, the playlist had a 'theme' to it. For instance, one week all of the songs may be singing about His Glory and another week all of the songs might have a cadence to them and sing of battles, wars, and victory. One week might find the songs singing about our need for Him. This week, however, the songs had to do with love. Love was what I craved and was crying out for more than anything. For the first time in my life I was in a place where I was able to see and understand that love was a good thing.

I would hear from others and see from the Word how love was what Jesus was all about. I knew that love had rescued me and was setting me free. I understood that love was supposed to be pure and safe and without condemnation. The only problem was that all of that regarding love was in my head and I needed the revelation of love in my heart. I wanted a supernatural understanding of how much Jesus loved me and what exactly love looked like.

About an hour into our worship time that Monday, I began to feel things in my body that I'd never felt before to this degree. I was over on the right side of the sanctuary, in front of the stage and on my knees. I had been lost in worship and just enjoying His Presence. The song 'Dance With Me' by

Robert Stearns began to play. As soon as the first word, 'Dance' was sung, I began to cry, but I didn't know why. I just felt like I was breaking inside. My upper arms began to feel numb and heavy all at once. Since then I've come to recognize that as a manifestation of His Presence in and on me. My belly began quivering in waves and I had that feeling you get right before you know that you are about to pass out. I laid face down on the floor, listening to the song and crying.

All of a sudden I saw myself standing in front of a ladder. I climbed up the ladder and at the top was about ten feet of golden carpet, almost as if it were lining a short walkway. I walked across the carpet and found myself at the foot of this enormously huge and wide spiral staircase. It was so large that I could not see the top of it. The steps were not just white, but a pure white. The banister of the staircase was decorated and engraved with gold and white going through it.

I heard a voice telling me to 'Come up here,' and I knew that I was supposed to walk up the spiral staircase. As I was walking up the stairs, I looked down at my clothes and it was as if my old clothes were being removed at the same time that a beautiful white dress was put on me. It was almost like a wedding gown, but it was the most incredible, beautiful, white dress and it ended before it got to my ankles. My body did not look like my body looks now. It was as if my body were a perfect size and weight and my hair was long.

At the top of the stairs it was as if I had entered the most incredible room that I'd ever been in. It was so amazing because of the brightness and reminded me of what I would assume a king's room would look like in a palace. The floor had these cobblestone bricks that were white yet clear. I could see light shining upward through the bricks. It looked like there were flecks of gold glitter sprinkled over them. There were beautiful golden leaves lying all over the room as if that were normal.

Far back to the left of the staircase was a small table that was draped with a white cloth. A large open book was on it that reminded me of a wedding guest book. A white feather was lying beside the book to write with. The book was white but the pages edges were outlined with gold. In front of and around the table was a golden braided cord that was looped in several places.

Towards the middle back of the room was a large chair that reminded me of the kind that kings would sit in. There was a large purple and golden cushion on the chair and the armrests, and the back of the chair had scrolls built into it. To the right of the chair was something that looked like an easel. It was filled with what looked like rolled up scrolls. They had gold on the edges and were tied with small golden ribbons.

A man came toward me with his hand outstretched. He was wearing white, but it was not an outfit that I was familiar with. There was gold engraved into his garments, and I realized that when the gold parts of his garment would hit the light, it made him appear illuminated. For some reason, even though I knew there was a man standing next to me and offering me his hand, I couldn't look at him. I just knew that there was this outstretched hand in front of me waiting for me to take it. I placed my hand in his and he turned and led me to another part of the room which had a bigger area. This area had the same flooring as the previous area that I had seen with the clear cobblestone bricks sprinkled with gold glitter. However, under these bricks it seemed as if water was flowing beneath them, as if we were standing on a sea of glass.

I heard the song 'Dance With Me' playing. The man and I were facing each other. I remember fighting the feeling of unworthiness, and my heart felt as if it was going to beat right out of my chest, but I still couldn't look him in the eyes. He then ever so gently took his hand and lifted my head up so I would see him. As soon as I did, I realized that it was Jesus. He placed his left hand into my right one, and he put his other hand on my left side. We began to dance. At first I pulled back and didn't want to dance with Him because I felt ashamed that I didn't know how to dance, at least not this kind of dance. Was this even right? No one had ever danced with me this way. I didn't even know what to do. But Jesus wouldn't let me pull back and the most amazing thing is that there was no way that I could have even if I wanted to.

As Jesus and I danced, He spoke four things to me. He told me how beautiful I was. He told me that I was clean and pure. He told me that He couldn't wait to dance with me. Then He told me that He loved me. It was so simple: 'I love you, Robin.' As soon as He said that, I looked into His eyes, and I was undone and consumed instantly by His love for me. I began to feel something happening inside of me that I'd never felt before. It was so incredible that I thought I would explode because it was coming from the inside out.

Those eyes! How can someone's eyes lead a dance? As I gazed into His eyes, I knew where to step, how to move, and how to follow His lead. It was effortless and nothing had to be said. How can it be that just looking into His eyes, I would become so wrecked by a love that was so deep and so encompassing that I felt consumed? I had never felt this kind of love before. The next closest thing to it was the love I had for my children. I could not quit looking into His eyes.

Here we were, Jesus and I dancing a dance, yet He was speaking to me, to my spirit with His eyes. It was as if looking into them was all that I needed. I felt a love and an intimacy that was so deep that it almost didn't make sense because it made it seem as if all that I'd learned and been taught about love and intimacy my whole life was barely touching what it really is in the kingdom of heaven. In my past and with various relationships, I had only known a love and intimacy with limits and oftentimes within those limits the intimacy was hindered, especially in the areas of sex, communication and expressing love. The love that I saw in Jesus's eyes destroyed the intimacy that my flesh knew, and it brought me into the intimacy of His heart.

The dance was almost over and I knew that I would be leaving, but I didn't want to leave His presence. I felt so safe, secure and protected. I felt cherished and adored. I felt chosen and beautiful. I could have stood there forever. As I looked once more into His eyes, He spoke love right back to me without speaking it out loud, and my heart received His love for me. I knew that from then on I could look into His eyes and run into His arms and dance with Him anytime I wanted. He had become the lover of my soul. I will never forget His eyes!"

That morning, Robin danced with the King of Glory. Holy Spirit had removed the veil of deception so she could see the truth, her answer, Jesus himself. Jesus was waiting for her all along up those stairs, and Robin could now hear His voice and answer His call to "come up here."

As she ascended the stairs she was clothed in

a beautiful white dress. Once face to face, Jesus lifted her head and she saw for herself that there was nothing she could do to keep her from His love. Through Him, she was completely accepted and worthy to be cherished. As she gazed into His eyes, she knew beyond a shadow of a doubt how the love of Jesus had rescued her from her deception.

Chapter Three

The Eyes of Fire

This incredible, intimate contact with Jesus encouraged Robin to continue her journey despite the continual attacks from the enemy. Because Robin was introduced into the occult as a young child, her inborn ability to sense the spiritual realm increased as she grew. By the time Robin had her dance with the King of Kings, she had been accustomed to seeing demonic forces, but now the truth, her Savior, was in clear view. She had caught a glimpse of Hell as well, but it was the love of her Savior that drew her and convinced her, not the fear. In her vision, it was the Savior's eyes that captivated her. At times, Robin also saw those "Jesus eyes" reflected through

It's Only A Shadow

Brandy. Robin recounted:

"When I first met Brandy, for some reason I never could look her in the eyes, even when we spoke. She scared me! I would look at her face, but I wouldn't look in her eyes. I just felt so much resistance to looking at her, and I was very uncomfortable.

When I scheduled my deliverance, my pastor told me that Brandy would be there to help. I was greatly opposed to having her there and asked him if it could be someone else besides her. He said, 'No, Brandy needs to be the one.' I even told him that I couldn't stand her looking at me. I told him that I felt judgment from her, and he let me know that I was wrong. I was in a battle all day just to get there for the deliverance. I'd feel panic, anger, and this fight inside of me that I was not familiar with.

On the night of my deliverance, Brandy

was already sitting in a chair in front of the couch when I got there. I could tell she smiled at me but I just looked past her and I took a seat on the couch where I would be as far from her as possible. After she prayed over our session, she began to talk to me and explain things that I never knew. As she talked, she kept reminding me to look into her eyes, and she would wait until I did. I had struggled my whole adult life with looking people in the eyes, but I never really knew why.

I know now that I didn't feel worthy, and I didn't want to feel condemned or rejected when people looked at me. I especially remember as a child not wanting people to hurt me by looking at me or to know what I was feeling or thinking by looking in my eyes. I learned very quickly to only glance at someone's eyes.

The first few times that Brandy had me

look at her as she spoke, I felt incredibly sick and wanted to run. I was in so much panic, and I did not feel safe.

For several hours each time that I'd look into her eyes to speak to Brandy or to hear what she had to say to me, I'd feel a challenge. I could feel myself staring into her eyes with defiance from mine, almost as if I was letting her know that she didn't have the upper hand!

We were into our last three hours of my deliverance when the battle of the eyes broke. Suddenly, I realized the eye contact was a good thing that pierced through to my thoughts and my heart. I began to feel safe instead of threatened, warmth instead of coldness. All anger and defiance left. There was something in those eyes that broke me out. They drew me, held me, and touched me like I'd never been touched before. That something was Jesus. I saw the love of Jesus coming down from Him and flowing through Brandy and out to me. I saw His eyes in her. I saw His love, His compassion, His justice, His pain and sorrow, His strength, but most of all it was His love.

Looking Brandy in the eyes was the most tangible encounter that I'd had with the love of Jesus. I also realized that when I gave Brandy eye contact, things in me broke and healing came more quickly. I didn't see the condemnation. I didn't feel the guilt or shame. Oh my, the love that she expressed to me because of Jesus overwhelmed me and undid me. All I knew was that I had to have more of this love.

As I have gone through more layers of deliverance, I've encountered many facets of those Jesus eyes through Brandy. Sometimes the eyes set me free, and other times they corrected me for coming against Brandy for the mandate she's been given from the

Lord. At times the eyes were piercing but in a different way, one with great authority that could communicate the seriousness of the matter.

I can remember one time when the enemy at work in me was challenging and opposing Brandy. She wasn't speaking to me but to what was at work in me. In other words she was speaking to the enemy coming out of me and opposing her. What was in me would try real hard to stay hidden and silent or would try to change tactics. Finally, Brandy had enough and told me to look at her. Then she gave me an ultimatum. All of a sudden it was as if her eyes flashed like lightening, and I literally felt the bolt of fire. All that was in me knew to stop doing what it was doing and to bow because the fire from heaven was right there. It caused all that was at work in me to be silenced. I began to confess what I needed to, and I quit changing tactics. All that was hidden came to light. The demonic knows who has authority.

As we've become friends and walked this out together, I can now look Brandy in the eyes all of the time. I still see the love of Jesus there, and at times I still get to witness the eyes of Jesus, the eyes of fire coming through her."

Looking deeply into someone else's eyes is very personal and intimate, and when doing so, there seems to be an exchange. In an exchange with the eyes, each sends and receives unspoken messages, and often there can be a sense of "knowing" of the other's intent. Brandy described:

> "The eyes are the light of the soul and through them we communicate our heart and thoughts. Therefore, whenever there is peace, joy, love, and acceptance within, the eyes seem to reflect that with a sense of love

and peace. When there is insecurity, fear, shame, or guilt, making eye contact with others can be difficult. It is easy for us to 'look down on' or condemn others with our eyes."

Communication through the eyes can have both evil and good intent. Robin had a keen awareness of the spiritual realm, so she was sensitive of this type of intimate communication.

Robin was schooled in spiritual tactics from childhood, and with trained acuity she keenly perceived spiritual realities typically experienced by most only in the conjured, fantasy movie realm. The spirits operating in Robin were repelled by the Jesus in Brandy and instinctively reacted. The eyes became a spiritual battlefront of opposing forces. At first, Robin translated the conflict in her mind as condemnation and judgment, but the love Brandy exuded broke the stalemate.

When the deception was lifted, Robin clearly

saw the blazing love and compassion in Brandy's eyes that reached through Brandy to grab hold of Robin. The love of Jesus is jealous and sometimes flares to break through any remaining resistant forces that opposed His work in His beloved. Robin distinguished the authority of Jesus in the combat zone of the eyes and dared not cross it; much like a child knows the limits of a loving father's stern look.

But what propels those who do not have Robin's experiences or spiritual eyes to seek the unseen realm? What causes one to persist in discovering the truths in an invisible reality when that reality is not clearly tangible? Second Corinthians 4:18 tells us to,

> "fix our eyes not on what is seen, but on what is unseen. For what is seen is temporary, but what is unseen is eternal."

And we are told in Matthew 6:19-21 (NLT),

> "Don't store up treasures here on earth, where they can be eaten by moths and get rusty, and where thieves break in and steal. Store your

treasures in heaven, where they will never become moth-eaten or rusty and where they will be safe from thieves. Wherever your treasure is, there your heart and thoughts will also be."
However, those admonishments, although clear enough, are often put aside when life in the natural extracts all of one's energies.

Nancy was entrenched in a respectable, normal, academic, and rational life. After her intense deliverance session, she had a choice to trust her perceptions and what had happened to her as real, or to deny both and slip back into her "normal." She could distance herself from Brandy or stick with her stand of faith. Although she perceived the spiritual realm and bought into an afterlife in that realm, she did not see evidence of it in her daily life. No one talked about it unless it was in relation to heaven, and that was a place to go upon death, not a place that was particularly relevant to life now. What would impel her to abandon traditional thinking about the reality of Kingdom of Heaven in the here and now and delve deeper into the supernatural sphere that consisted of both light and dark powers?

In Nancy's church, there was no extensive talk of spirits of any kind, and casting out demons was only considered applicable to the apostles in a different church age. Nancy had no frame of reference to deal with her own body writhing like a snake. Why didn't she bolt and run after such a vivid encounter with the demonic?

Deep within her spirit Nancy knew her perception of a reality outside the natural rang true, but she had no concrete evidence and no knowledge confirming the existence of the heavenly realm in the here and now, not yet. To the contrary, she had a mistrust of all things supernatural shared by virtually all of her friends, family, and church, so she grouped all mystical things into the paranormal realm, which she considered evil and with which she wanted no contact.

Although the commissioning words of Jesus to "heal the sick, raise the dead, and cast out demons" tugged on Nancy's sensibilities, she had no concept those words applied to her and no contact with any good power that could do that, until her own deliverance from an evil force that pulsed through her very own body. Fear may have kept her on the road to discovery at first, but it was a series of subsequent events that would inevitably convince her. One of those events was staged in the unseen plane when she saw those "Jesus eyes" through Brandy.

It was in a subsequent round of deliverance with Brandy when Nancy was again completely caught off guard. She recalled:

> "I don't even remember what my issue in the deliverance was. We successfully dealt with the issue, and after prayer as we were closing up, I remember looking up into Brandy's eyes and gasping for breath. Of course I see Brandy's eyes all of the time, but this time caught me totally off guard. I am not sure I knew at the time I was looking

into the eyes of Jesus, but my spirit understood and connected beyond my conscious level.

I felt like I was drawn into infinity. All I can describe is a depth that just kept going and going. I saw it with my own eyes. It looked like you might imagine deep space, moving with shades of blue. I haven't seen anything like it before or since. I was suspended and felt connected at a deep level to a love that picked me up, held me tight, and drew me in. It captured me in something beyond myself. I felt secure and comfortable, yet bewildered because it was so extraordinary. As suddenly as it began, it ended, and even to this day I am at a loss to describe what I saw reflected from Brandy's eyes. Because Christ lives in all of us, I can only imagine I caught a glimpse of Christ in Brandy. It was real and tangible and I saw it. I will never be the same. I can't go back."

Paul writes in Colossians 1:26-27,

> "the mystery that has been kept hidden for ages and generations, but is now disclosed to the saints. To them God has chosen to make known among the Gentiles the glorious riches of this mystery, which is Christ in you, the hope of glory."

Was it the "hope of glory" that drove Brandy to spend an incredible amount of her time and energies pulling captives from their prison cells? Did she know when she reflected "Jesus eyes?" Had she seen those eyes through someone else? Was that enough for her?

The enemy resisted Brandy relentlessly to try to force her to stop, so why did she continue? What made her persevere? What made her prioritize the freedom of others, many times above her own family? What kept her going?

In her own words, Brandy stated her mission:

"My heart is to see the body of Christ, the bride, encounter God's presence daily through absolute surrender to the Holy Spirit and out of this love relationship, bring heaven to earth, just as Jesus did through the anointing of the Holy Spirit. I desire to see the kingdom of God established through every believer as they receive freedom and come into their callings and destinies and receive revelation of who their God is and who they are in Christ.

I want to see strong prophetic worshippers, warriors, and revivalists raised up and sent out with authority, empowered by God to their spheres of influence; to gather in a harvest of harvesters and to bring in the lost, in obedience to Jesus' words in Matthew 28:19 go and 'make disciples of all the nations,' and Mathew 10:7 (NKJV) 'As you go, preach, saying, 'The kingdom of heaven is at hand.' Heal the sick, cleanse the lepers, raise the dead, cast out demons. Freely you've received, freely give.'"

However the enemy was, in Robin's words, "stirred up" against Brandy's mission. Brandy needed to encounter for herself the many facets of the burning love of Jesus in order to endure the vicious fight that was unfolding. Every aspect of Brandy's life would be attacked repeatedly, including her family, her ministry, her character, and her own body. She clung to the Apostle John's description of Jesus in Revelations 1:12-16:

> "I turned around to see the voice that was speaking to me. And when I turned I saw seven golden lampstands, and among the lampstands was someone 'like a son of man,' dressed in a robe reaching down to his feet and with a golden sash around his chest. His head and hair were white like wool, as white as snow, and his eyes were like blazing fire. His feet were like bronze glowing in a furnace, and his voice was like the

sound of rushing waters. In his right hand he held seven stars, and out of his mouth came a sharp double-edged sword. His face was like the sun shining in all its brilliance."

After beholding Jesus, John "fell at his feet like as though dead." His description of Jesus' eyes was "like blazing fire," and the picture was one of a burning, piercing, red-hot desire. Jesus's love has been described as a jealous love, so His eyes blaze vehemently with a protective passion as He pursues mankind and His bride. Because of the resistance Brandy faced when she moved into the territory, she needed to receive the revelation of God's love and Christ's perseverance as in 2 Thessalonians 3:5 so that she could endure. She described what she experienced:

> "Before moving here, I never faced any real persecution for my faith, just disagreements here and there. Our greatest heartbreak was the change of vision within the

local church we had been in for years before we moved here. In that church we were on full time staff only a year before the leadership changed their minds and we had to find work again outside of the church. Due to this we had to leave our church family and close relationships with friends as the Lord opened up work for us. All doors were shut for any work where we were, and it had never even entered our minds that we would have to move. We had raised our six children there, and leaving was one of the most difficult things we had ever done. The Lord assured me, 'Did I not say to you if you believe, you will see the glory of God?' (John 11:40, NASV).

Once we came here, we quickly joined another church, and over time we received healing from the loss of close relationships and family. We just gave life, ministered, and formed new relationships. After a year and a half, however, the ministry of deliverance we had started came under fire. I was asked by the pastors to stop ministering in deliverance and was told what books I could teach out of within their church and that our visions were different. I stood on the word of God in Acts 4:19-20 (NKJV) where the disciples were told to stop preaching Jesus. Their response became mine. 'Whether it is right in the sight of God to listen to you more than to God, you judge. For we cannot but speak the things which we have seen and heard.' So, we left that fellowship and suffered loss of relationships due to our stand for truth and obedience to God's word. "

Devastated by the break with this church and hindered from the freedom to express all that God had called her to be, Brandy told the Lord, "I am not going back to a local church unless you show me the name of a church on a banner in front of me."

As a result, she stayed home on Sundays and worshiped there. During that period, Brandy and the Lord became very intimate, and she characterized this time as "being baptized into His love." Through reading the bible, seeking Jesus, and worshipping Him, Brandy was taken to a whole new level in her relationship. Jesus became her everything. She found herself with a new understanding of Song of Solomon 4:9 (NKJV),

> "You have ravished my heart with one look of your eyes."

She understood what it did to the Lord when she turned her gaze towards him and found that it overtook Him, so much so that He says in Song of Solomon 6:5 (NKJV),

> "Turn your eyes from me; they overwhelm me."

Brandy understood that the Lord opened up His heart to the one who cried out for Him. She focused on His love as in Song of Solomon 8:6-7,

> "Place me like a seal over your heart, like a seal on your arm; for love is as strong as death, its

jealousy unyielding as the grave. It burns like blazing fire, like a mighty flame. Many waters cannot quench love; rivers cannot wash it away. If one were to give all the wealth of his house for love, it would be utterly scorned."

Brandy began to grasp the all-consuming love that conquered death and pursued her. However, this understanding was in her head. What she really needed was a true revelation of those truths for herself. As she continued to seek, love was revealed to her, and she recalled that pivotal point:

"For the first time in my life I felt like it was just Jesus and I. Hurting from the abandonment of loved ones that I once had fellowship with, I felt all alone in the journey. I felt myself losing hope. One day I was in my bathroom putting on my makeup. I had been spending time with the Lord and expressing my heart. I ended up weeping and crying out to God as I told Him I just didn't think I could take any more pain.

Suddenly, I turned around and Jesus was standing right there in the Spirit. His words to me were, 'Brandy, I am right here.' I fell to my face at His feet and worshiped Him. I felt like the woman in the bible who washed Jesus's feet with her tears and dried them with her hair. When you see Him, when you know that He is there, when you feel His presence, and when you encounter His voice, you won't do anything but fall to the ground and worship. You lay low and exalt your king. The words He spoke to me have carried me through.

Second Timothy 4:17,18 (NASV) has new meaning for me,

> 'But the Lord stood with me and strengthened me, so that through me the proclamation might be fully accomplished, and that all the Gentiles might hear; and I was rescued out of the lion's mouth. The

Lord will rescue me from every evil deed, and will bring me safely to His heavenly kingdom; to Him be the glory forever and ever. Amen.' "

In the days following this encounter, Brandy sought more. Brandy had been baptized and filled with Holy Spirit, she had known Holy Spirit, but she wanted more of Holy Spirit. She wanted to know the depth and height and width and length of the Lord's love. So she prayed Ephesians 1: 17-23, over herself:

"I keep asking that the God of our Lord Jesus Christ, the glorious Father, may give you the Spirit of wisdom and revelation, so that you may know him better. I pray also that the eyes of your heart may be enlightened in order that you may know the hope to which he has called you, the riches of his glorious inheritance in the saints, and his incomparably great power for us who believe.

That power is like the working of his mighty strength, which he exerted in Christ when he raised him from the dead and seated him at his right hand in the heavenly realms, far above all rule and authority, power and dominion, and every title that can be given, not only in the present age but also in the one to come. And God placed all things under his feet and appointed him to be head over everything for the church, which is his body, the fullness of him who fills everything in every way."

Brandy asked for the Spirit of Wisdom and Revelation to come to her and open the eyes of her understanding to reveal Jesus to her. When she did, she was caught up into a vision. She described it:

"I actually saw myself sitting on a beach facing the ocean. It was so peaceful, and the sounds of the waves seemed to roll over me as I sat in the stillness. I knew the ocean was likened unto the revelations of God – so endless and vast; so deep - and like the waves that relentlessly and continually break into the beach, so His revelation of His love rolled over me. I literally felt wisdom and revelation (Isaiah 11:2) awaken me and open my spiritual eyes to know and see in the spirit. For the first time I understood that heaven and earth were connected, and heaven was open to me through Jesus Christ!

My understanding just became His. I could see with His understanding. I saw the Lord's eyes. I was receiving understanding of what the Lord Jesus saw and perceived. The eyes of my understanding just came in line with His. Now I knew why He pursues us all, and that burning passion was given to me for others. My imagination had opened up to the Spirit of wisdom and revelation, to know Him! (Ephesians 1:18)

I was taken to a whole new level in revelation, a whole new place from ground level to up onto the heavens where we are seated with Christ in heavenly places, far above all rule, power, authority, and dominion. My eyes were opened and I could see from a third heaven perspective where I was always placed from the very beginning. I could see, hear, feel, and encounter God in a new relationship in the spirit.

After this time, my dreams and visions escalated. I had already been having dreams where the Lord would reveal Himself to me at different times in many ways. I was acquainted with the casting out of demons and healing and doing miracles in my dreams, but now it changed. I was having glory dreams and encounters with the Lord on a weekly basis. I saw the angelic and the glory of the Lord! I was escalated and taken up.

I had never in all my life experienced such love and peace! My relationship with Holy Spirit was totally transformed as it became so real and personal. I seemed to live in a state of 'bliss' and I was 'lovesick' for Jesus!"

After six months had passed, one morning as Brandy's family gathered for their time with Jesus, the Lord gave Brandy another open vision:

"I was sitting on the couch in worship and all of a sudden I saw a vision before my eyes. I saw a banner with the name of a church on it, and with it I heard the Lord's voice, 'I want you to return to the local church. No longer consider unclean what I have made clean.' (Acts 10:15) All I could do was say, 'Yes, Lord!' I repented of my pride that prompted me to speak such brash words to the Father of what I would not do, but He honored my request and came just the way I asked. HE so loves His Bride!"

Brandy and her family did go to another church soon after that, but she spent an entire year doing nothing but simply attending the service on Sunday mornings. A few months later, Brandy joined friends at a conference, in another city and while there, she received a fresh new impartation and anointing to desire to know what would please her King! She fell in love all over again!

How much love do you want? How much revelation of Jesus can you have? Will He ever stop revealing it to an individual who seeks Him? Would He ever say, "NO", to that child? Never!

Brandy had revelation of the physical presence of the Lord Jesus, but while at this conference she had the privilege of seeing His eyes through someone else. She recounted this incredible experience:

"While at the conference, my friend was as

desperate as I was to know and to encounter Jesus! Encounter Him he did! My friend was suddenly caught up in the spirit, seeing with the 'eyes of understanding' and beholding the glory of the Lord! He described it as only experiencing a 'teaspoon full' out of a 'sea of glory'! He was unable to even walk by himself, much less sit up straight. During this remarkable encounter, he would pray in his heavenly language, communing with the Spirit of Truth, and he could see everything 'as it really was'. All things were open and laid bare. His wife and I watched in amazement and listened intently! I will never forget when he turned to us with his eyes opened for the first time after having gone into the spirit, and when he looked at us, we were overcome with awe, as we both said at the same time, 'He has Jesus eyes!' They burned with fire. They burned with passion. They seemed to burn right through us both! I had never seen those eyes ablaze in any person before!

I would see those eyes again through him later in my journey. Once, when he and I were praying for Robin after she had a horrific attack from Satan, Robin and I both looked up into his eyes and saw the eyes of justice and judgment. The fear of the Lord flooded our souls, and we were both captivated with a King – Jesus – who had revealed Himself yet again to us both in a way that we had never seen as He destroyed the works of the devil!

'For the Lord your God is a consuming fire, a jealous God' (Deuteronomy 4:24).

'Therefore understand today that the Lord your God is He who goes before you as a consuming fire. He will destroy them and bring them down before you; so you shall drive them out and destroy them quickly, as the Lord has said to you' (Deuteronomy 9:3, NKJV).

Upon another occasion, we were praying for Robin at my friend's home, and the Lord had chosen that night, in the midst of high level warfare and freedom, to come to me to set me apart and anoint me, and set me into the apostolic office.

'It was he who gave some to be apostles, some to be prophets, some to be evangelists, and some to be pastors and teachers' (Ephesians 4:11).

I stopped in the middle of Robin's deliverance session as I could hear the Holy Spirit speak softly to me to be quiet and still. I felt as if all strength had been drained out of me. I fell to my face and started repenting for trying to do things in my own strength. I prayed for a while. Then I finally got up, and to my surprise my friend had left the room and had just returned with anointing oil. I looked up into his eyes, and there Jesus was again! I melted as His eyes pierced through to my heart and soul with such love, and purpose as he spoke, 'It is time!'

Knowing I was called to the apostolic office through a word of the Lord given to me a year prior to this time, I embraced quickly the Lord's choosing of me. Great joy and happiness filled me! I saw Jesus as my great High Priest, the Apostle of my faith!

'Therefore, holy brethren, partakers of a heavenly calling, consider Jesus, the Apostle and High Priest of our confession;' (Hebrews 3:1, KJV).

By the laying on of hands, I was set apart and commissioned privately, as were Barnabas and Saul in Acts 13:2-3,

'While they were worshiping the Lord and fasting, the Holy Spirit said, 'Set apart for me Barnabas and Saul for the work to which I have called them.'

So after they had fasted and prayed, they placed their hands on them and sent them off.

Such anointing and power flowed through my being, and I felt a whole new strength. Now I understood – the strength I needed was indeed God given authority to do His will!

> 'Blessed is the man whose strength is in you, whose heart is set on a pilgrimage. As they pass through the Valley of Baca [weeping], they make it a spring; the rain also covers it with pools. They go from strength to strength; each one appears before God in Zion' (Psalms 84:5-7, NKJV).

Seeing Jesus in others is so real and defining. Jesus Himself said,

> 'He who has seen me has seen the Father;' (John 14:9 NKJV).

> 'Assuredly, I say to you, inasmuch as you did it to one of the least of these my breth-

ren, you did it to me' (Mathew 25:40 NKJV).

Revelation of Jesus Christ! This is the answer for all who seek truth, love, and restoration! Beautiful Holy Spirit brings the manifest presence to those who love Him and obey Him according to Jesus' own words,

'At that day you will know that I am in My Father, and you in Me, and I in you. He who has My commandments and keeps them, it is he who loves Me. And he who loves Me will be loved by My Father, and I will love him and manifest Myself to him' (John 14:20-21, NKJV).

Fire purges, cleanses, purifies, and goes to the depth of who you are."

Brandy received the strength and vision that it would take for her to persevere through the onslaught of attacks that would follow. She saw the eyes of fire for herself and that was enough for her to continue.

Chapter Four

Prophetic Warrior

It was a Sunday night meeting of the group assembled around Brandy's mission. The gathering started with an opening prayer, followed by communion and a powerful worship time led by a prophetic band. Brandy was standing facing the band at the front, Nancy was behind her to her left, and Robin was flanking her right.

Others had gravitated to their usual positions in the front as well, and all were engaging in radical worship. The meetings were noted and sometimes criticized for demonstrative displays of praise, so an uninhibited, expressive show of lifted hands adoring the King and jubilant dancing in response to freedom was normal, not the exception.

The weight of the Presence of the Lord began to permeate the atmosphere during worship. Nancy felt it and struggled to stand. Normally she closed her eyes to focus on her own worship, but this night she kept a watchful eye in the natural. Suddenly, Nancy saw Brandy become still after swaying in concert with the music and then bow to an unseen being that seemed to be standing in front of her. Barely able to stay upright in the weighty presence but eager not to miss anything, Nancy strained to perceive what was going on in the spiritual dimension facing Brandy.

Suddenly Nancy knew. Jesus was there, in person, right there in front of Brandy. Nancy's inkling was confirmed when Brandy began nodding her head up and down and whispering, "Yes Lord." As Brandy bowed lower and lower with her hands stretched out to her side, Nancy followed suit.

Most of the others had continued in their

personal worship, and the band eventually finished the songs they had planned. Reverently, Brandy laid down on the carpet, and as she often did when the Presence descended, she invited others to join her in the glory.

Nancy stretched out close to where Brandy was. Soon, Brandy motioned for someone to put on music from her iPod to protect the spiritual flow that had started and continued honoring the glory presence. Holy Spirit directed her to play the *Prophetic Warrior* CD, a powerful instrumental by John Belt. The sound of the drums on the opening track, *Prepare for War*, sent Nancy into a vivid vision.

Nancy had listened to the *Prophetic Warrior* CD consistently for well over two years on her morning walks, and when she did, incredible previews of spiritual battles concerning the movement of God in the territory flooded her perception. In her words:

"The Prophetic Warrior CD is a powerful instrumental that draws on drums and cymbals to tell a story of war. The tracks alternate the beat between thundering attack rhythms, flowing melodies depicting the calm between confrontations, and resounding victory anthems. It calls forth visions of rising and ebbing battle scenes. However, for me, this CD is more than inspirational music to help me exercise; it is the backdrop for revelations concerning a sovereign move of God happening in my midst. It is a window into the spiritual dimension."

The more Nancy listened to the CD, the more she became sensitive to what she felt Holy Spirit was saying concerning God's move in the territory. She was given certain scriptures to declare during certain parts of the CD, and she kept a journal of revelations she received concerning spiritual warfare she was detecting. She wrote:

"As the music played today, I recited the Lord's Prayer, and when I said, 'Your Kingdom Come,' the word, kingdom, resonated in my soul like an earthquake that starts at the epicenter and moves out across the adjoining terrain. The victory with Robin [the day the axe fell] was a major miracle. She was freed from the tight grip of the enemy through generations who participated in occultism. God is moving in signs and wonders in our very midst, establishing His Kingdom here in direct conflict with the kingdom that, to this date, has been in power. As God's Kingdom advances, His Domain will begin to change the landscape of the city through the people He is freeing.

I was sobered by the fact that there are precious few of us who have any frame of reference for what is really happening in the spiritual realm, and most people are unaware of the reality of the spiritual battle over this region. Those embroiled in the evil are painfully aware, but the rest of the people are cloaked in many forms of disbelief ranging from a flagrant unbelief that the spiritual world exists to merely separating spiritual things from day-to-day activities. The enemy is counting on unbelief to neutralize the opposition.

We are engaged in one fierce battle after another. The warning for me is that the extent to which I recognize and value the spiritual realm is the extent to which the Kingdom will be released through me. Otherwise, I will not recognize the legions of angels that are assigned to me, much less release them into any of my battles to war on my behalf."

The warfare Nancy sensed became regular scenes playing on the big screen of her mind's eye with the CD as the accompanying sound track. In the spirit, she regularly saw warriors donning medieval armor before daybreak, gathering around a massive fire to plan their attack, mounting horses poised for battle, and thunderously riding into battle, each rider followed by personal scores of angels fanned out behind. She began referring to these scenes as "the movie." From her journal she described the reccurring sequence of events:

> "In the movie this morning, we gathered around the campfire as dawn was breaking, awaiting the arrival of each member of the team. The sky was dark blue with clouds hovering, and from our vantage point on the hill I could see a massive expanse of territory before us. As I moved through the scene, different people were putting on helmets, buckling boots, adjusting armor, and gathering spears and shields. Today it was clear that this battle belonged to King Jesus. We have been shown battle fronts and we have seen the enemy's plans, but we will not be

orchestrating the battles. Jesus will. It will not be fought in the manner we envision. It is a spiritual battle and will unfold beyond our expectations.

Soon we all mounted our horses and tried to contain them as they were pitching and surging with power. I could smell the might in the air and could feel the intensity of the moment as adrenaline rushed through my body and conviction swelled in my spirit. I could taste the tang of certain victory.

Although the time of day was different, it was a scene much like the one in **Braveheart** where the troops lined up on horses and Mel Gibson rode back and forth in front of the line shaking his sword to fire up the warriors. Today, I was among many in the ranks. I knew Jesus was there as our commander, but I couldn't see Him in the distance. Our leaders were conferring while we strained to hold back our horses.

The moment came when we were released. We flooded down the hill headed to the battlefield which took on a supernatural appearance. There were visible dragons and demons to slay, and they had names such as fear, jealousy, rage, abandonment, and addiction. Although they seemed formidable, our victory was certain because the power we wielded was absolute, decisive, and sufficient.

Today, I was both riding and watching at the same time because as we took off, I seemed to ascend to catch an aerial view. I could hear the thunder of power as our army rode in a V-shaped formation, and fanning out above each warrior in a smaller V-shape was a regimen of angels. I couldn't see the end of the angels, as their number couldn't be counted. It was a massive scene.

Later, warriors broke off into different directions and took charge of the angelic forces behind them, engaging the enemy in their respective paths. My vantage point switched from warrior to warrior as I saw them each fighting for personal freedom. At this point each warrior was on his or her own personal battleground with angelic reinforcements. For many, each swing of the sword dealt complete destruction as the warriors along with the angels never broke stride.

However, there was a slow point in the cadence on the CD where I saw a particular warrior on a horse rare up in slow motion. The battle was very intense and it was as if my perception froze to focus on this warrior. I sensed the extreme cost to the warrior, and I saw flashbacks in rapid succession of many previous bloody battles. I wondered if he or she would make it this time. At other times I have seen myself on my own horse, and I recalled the losses I suffered in my own journey.

At one point, those who made it through

their own personal battlegrounds gathered to survey the remaining terrain while others were still battling. Those who were victorious thus far took off again. They looked like highly trained athletes at peak performance, operating in the 'zone' with perfect precision of movement.

After a considerable battle, I was among those who made it through the combat zone today, and we ended up in the meadowlands to take a rest. We got off our horses and moved to the lush green fields, sweating from the intensity of the battle. It didn't take long to catch our breath, and before I knew it we were sitting at a commissioning table, feasting and awaiting further orders. There was great camaraderie around the table as we exchanged stories, laughing and toasting to our victory.

The word trickled down through the warriors seated at the table that we would be returning to battle soon, but this time it would be in the natural not the supernatural battlefield. On that battlefield there will be no grand display of power, and no visible dragons to slay. We will have assumed our normal identities and will operate under cover in the natural realm. Still equipped with our spiritual amour and angelic reinforcements, we will be able to move through this combat zone with our appearance as warriors and spirit-given motives largely undetected. We are equipped with a stealth covering, and the enemy will be unsuspecting of our battle plan. We are still at full war, but the battleground changes."

So, first the warriors battled openly on a personal, supernatural battleground where the spirits with which they struggled were visible. Once they gained freedom, were equipped, and became successful with supernatural tactics, they were commissioned to covertly go into the natural world. This lined up with what was happening around Nancy. Brandy prayed with many, including Nancy, who became aware of spiritual warfare and won personal freedom on the deliverance battleground. Brandy's ultimate mission was to follow what Jesus said to do in setting up God's government in the territory and bring the Kingdom of Heaven to earth as it is in Heaven.

From time to time, different parts of "the movie" sequence were highlighted in greater detail for further revelation. For example, one day Nancy received revelation on about how pain is turned into authority and power in spiritual warfare. She described:

> "It is clear to me that the battlefield in which we each ride is somehow connected to the pain we have experienced in our lives. That pain must be exchanged for power. I have a choice in dealing with the trauma and

pain I experience. If I don't deal with it, it becomes a weakness for me when I fight. I have been delivered from trauma and pain, but I must deliberately lay it down along with the shame and not let it define me. Once I do that, I convert the pain into power and authority to battle. The choice to lay pain down became apparent to me today.

The extent of the pain I encounter may indeed define the power and authority in which I operate. The adage, 'No pain no gain' holds a lot of truth in the spiritual realm. For example, I can operate in a battle against abandonment and betrayal because I have authority there. I have experienced a divorce and have gained authority in that particular arena. I have been delivered from the pain associated with the divorce by the suffering Jesus experienced. I do not have to carry it - He already did. I can choose to be yoked by it or exchange it for the yoke of Jesus. His burdens are light. I choose to lay down the pain and the shame associated with the pain, even the memory of the pain, and in doing so, I convert it into power in the arena of abandonment and betrayal.

In the battlefield, I can validate the pain of others who are experiencing abandonment and betrayal, and I have authority to fight the demons associated with it because I carry that authority. Today it was apparent that I needed to explore the battlegrounds in which I have access to authority so I can fight effectively."

Often, the movie seemed to be interactive instead of repetitive, with changes in the scenes corresponding to natural events as time went by. Nancy saw more and more familiar faces in the morning movie, and what she saw proved to be prophetic at times. For example, Nancy knew when an emerging alliance with a new member of the team was completed by whether or not she saw the member gather on the spiritual frontline.

Nancy also noticed a particularly sticky battlefield positioned like fly paper just as the warriors emerged from their own personal combat zones. In the spirit, this region served as a final proving ground that delayed and often stopped warriors from moving forward on the mission. In the natural it was a place where the enemy used all kinds of last-ditch tactics to delay, to cause fear, or lay an Achilles heel trap.

At times soldiers would move through this area with ease, but at other times they would fall prey to the snares and get stuck. Because it was strategically positioned right before the warriors emerged victoriously from their own battles, it was the final barrier that stood in the way of them realizing their destinies and taking their positions at the commissioning table.

A particularly common tactic Satan used on this battlefield was to set a fire among personalities to get them to take offense with one another. The goal was to separate the person holding the offense from the pack with self-righteous indignation. Nancy found herself seriously struggling with a contentious situation that developed among the team Brandy assembled. She felt like she was in that sticky place herself, but fortunately she received revelation of the nature of this battleground before she became a casualty to it. She explained:

> "The enemy set a fire among the leadership team Brandy assembled. Like most fires, it started out small but it flared into a furnace that now may endanger the entire mission. The issue wasn't even an issue that concerned me, but I spoke up with good intentions of trying to help. Now one thing led to another and there are lots of offenses in the group. Brandy stepped in to arbitrate and destroy the forces at work, and now all I hear in my mind is 'I have done nothing wrong and I

am being misunderstood.' I feel stuck and victimized.

I know in these situations I need to look at my error first to see where I am at fault, but for the life of me I can't see what I did wrong. I started my morning walk today in confusion, and I was in the middle of it when all of sudden in a split second, the veil of present reality dropped for me, much like it had done in a few precious moments in the past. For a nanosecond, I was literally and totally in a spiritual landscape. I was on a battlefield, one I have seen before. Today, though, it looked bigger, more panoramic.

I saw myself lift my head out of a trench to sense my surroundings. In the distance, I saw a vast military movement, and I heard bombs going off all around me. It was like a World War II movie where the troops were slowly moving forward while bombs were going off all around. I looked around to see if there was anyone around me, but I didn't see anyone. I felt lost. I knew beyond a shadow of a doubt that this was a very dangerous place to be. I felt the fear of the Lord and did not want to be in this place without protection or out of order. I somehow knew I needed to be in alignment with the authority that had set me in that place.

Then I saw the name hovering over the trench in which I was hiding. It was labeled, 'Good Intentions.' As long as I was inside this trench, I could not see clearly. I had to get out of the trench to restore my vision. It took all the courage I had but I finally crawled out of it.

When I emerged, I immediately heard the word, authority, and then I was immediately taken to the very gruesome scene at the cross where all authority was regained by my precious Savior, Jesus. I could hear the words, 'All authority has been given to Me in heaven and on earth' (Matthew 28:18-19, NKJV). I looked up and all I could see was the bloody body of Jesus hanging on the cross. I'm not sure I can even describe what I saw or felt. Words pale when you find yourself at the foot of Jesus at the cross. I am forever changed. The word, authority, will forever bring up that vivid image of the cross for me.

And then, as quickly as the revelation of the cross came, the scene changed and I could see Jesus setting Brandy in authority. It was like He was passing a baton to her, and she was given authority for this spiritual battleground on which I was standing. I had willfully joined her mission, and therefore I was under her authority. I needed to be in order. Authority was my protection. She was leading the charge of the movement I could see in the distance.

From that moment, the twisted path I had

been on seemed to straighten. In stepping out of the 'good intentions' trench, I could retrace my steps from a different perspective. From where I was standing now, I recognized many who were still hiding in deceit in those 'good intentions' trenches. I knew how it felt while in there and knew the fear and lies that accompanied me in the trench. It grieved me to know I had been there, but I was glad I could now see more clearly.

As I retraced the events that had taken place, it was clear how the enemy had set a fire in our camp. He fanned the flame until the fire drew the team around it. However, from this perspective, I could see that this fire was only part of the strategy. The real intent was to destroy the movement and take out the leadership. The fire was just a method to draw the team in. It wasn't about the fire or the issue at hand; it was about what damage could be inflicted through it. The enemy started the fire in the contention he crafted within the team. As I approached the fire, I fell into a 'good intentions' trench and brought with me more of my 'stuff.' As a result, I became battle worn and distracted with personal issues.

Like the Ghost of Christmas Past took Ebenezer Scrooge to events in his past, Holy Spirit took me back to the meeting where the fire was first started. He revealed to me how my one 'well-meaning' comment had been used to undermine authority in the situation. He then proceeded to show me the progression of how hiding in the trench of 'good intentions' left me prey to a very crooked path of thinking and justification. Needless to say, I was as horrified at this revelation as Scrooge was at his.

Intention is defined in the dictionary as mentally determining the purpose or attitude behind an action. In other words, I can have in my mind either a good or bad intention behind what I am doing or saying. Furthermore, intentions have value placed on them by the same mind that engineered them. This tends to result in justification of our words or actions based on what we *intended* instead of actual results.

In my case, I decided that because I had no bad intentions, I was not wrong. I did not have to focus on the truth of what I said because I meant no harm. In this thought path, if someone else takes exception to my 'well-meaning' comment, or if things go bad in the situation, I have no part in the blame. I am tempted to take up an alliance with the victim mentality, seeing myself in the situation as innocent and others as the perpetrators.

My thought process went like this – I was attacked unjustifiably as a result of an innocent comment. I have been misunderstood; therefore, I will either mistrust or withdraw myself from the person or group who would do something like that to me. Meanwhile, I remain unrepentant because I am hiding in the trench and I meant no harm. The offense stands and so does the breach in the relationship.

I saw that the breach in the relationship was the enemy's goal, not the issue at hand. What is really scary is how well it worked! The team that was once comprised of strong relationships was suddenly clouded with mistrust and misunderstanding. Because I felt victimized, my connection to the team was like a house of cards that began to fall. I was on the brink of removing myself from the team and the mission.

By the grace of God, I was shown that intentions do not matter on this sticky battlefield. What matters is the truth. Intentions are conjured up in the mind, justified by that same mind, and cloud any wisdom that can be brought to the situation. Armed with this understanding, I stepped out of the trench and repented quickly. Almost as fast as the fire was started, it was put out. Thank God I made it through that last sticky plain full of good intentions trenches."

As the enemy often does when he is facing an advancing army, he tried to start a fight between the members of the team, urging someone to take offense so he could divide the troops. It was no wonder that this battlefield was the last one before the warriors were commissioned for the dangerous covert ops. Only one who can put the truth above his or her feelings and intentions can be trusted to carry out such missions. Once Nancy became aware of this combat zone, she began seeing more and more people who had previously emerged to sit at the table get stuck and fall prey in that final, treacherous field.

That Sunday night, when the *Prophetic Warrior* CD started playing, it was as if the movie began

It's Only A Shadow

again and played for the first time for Nancy. The drums were fresh and echoed with a new vibrancy. Already on the floor, Nancy sensed the presence of the King of Glory in the very room close to where she was lying. It was as if two years of previous prophecy had caught up to the present and, like dominoes, fell one-by-one into the reality of the moment. What was so vivid to her in the past just got stunningly more intense. Nancy described:

> "The Presence was gloriously heavy, and I knew Jesus was physically in the room. I perceived He was standing in front of Brandy, speaking to her. I so wanted to touch the hem of His garment! Shock waves of heaven invading earth literally hit me in the stomach and I crunched as they doubled me over. Then I heard the opening drums of *Prophetic Warrior*. It was if what I had seen in the past was literally happening in the present. All of the revelations came together in illuminated

clarity. The intensity overwhelmed me, and I felt like I was immersed in the reality of the spiritual realm overlapping the natural.

I felt like I was in the midst of the movie I had seen so many times in the past. It was if I had just seen portions of the movie before, trailers, but now I was in the middle of the movie with surround sound in full blast. My senses were on overload. During the first track of the CD, I felt like I was actually putting on my armor and gathering with the others around me. It was surreal.

When we were gathered around the fire before we mounted our horses, I broke out in loud tongues. At the top of my lungs I was decreeing war cries from my spirit. I felt the passion of the Lord burn for His people in this territory. I felt the literal fire of His heart in the room, and I knew He was here in our midst about to lead the charge.

Then we mounted our horses and exploded

into battle. There are no words to describe what I felt. Bolts were shooting through my body, and I hung on in the natural to what was thundering in the spirit.

The battle was fierce and then the moment of truth came for me. The music slowed, and it was if I had fallen in my own personal battleground, mortally wounded with the collective pain of all my personal battles. I had battled for and lost twin granddaughters to miscarriage, suffered debilitating attacks on my physical body, endured the loss of my closest friends, born wounds of ridicule from the unbelief of friends and family, and taken the wrath of offenses from blinded comrades. The King Himself walked over to me and held me. In His hands He took all of the deep wounds that had been inflicted, both spiritually and physically, and pulled them out of my bloody body in an astounding exchange. There are no words to describe the way I felt in His arms.

Then in the natural, Robin went over and grabbed a flag and waved it over me. With each whoosh over my shaking body, my wounds were being healed. I was mortally wounded on the battlefield, and Jesus was there to pick me up. He held me and took my injuries and as He did, Robin laid the flag over me. I was uncontrollably sobbing, and I felt the supernatural healing of my Savior along with the overwhelming support of my fellow warrior. Once again, there are no words.

As I was lying there, it felt like Jesus went from warrior to warrior in the spiritual plain, picking up the pieces and making exchanges, their pain for His Glory. Then my focus turned again to Robin. I saw her standing there in the spirit on the battleground. It was like she had seen me lying on the ground and had gotten off her horse to give me a hand.

When she saw I was okay she mounted her horse and rode off. Renewed in strength and in spirit, I arose and faced the oncoming enemy. I felt I could supernaturally defend against anything the enemy could throw at me. I did not see anything, but I could hear the bombs going off and the artillery fire increase. I was back on my feet.

What I perceived was the spiritual battle in which we were embroiled at the moment in following the mission set before Brandy. The battle was real, perfectly clear and intensely fierce. I know Jesus Himself came to me and literally made an exchange of His strength for my pain. I received strength to continue on the mission which was clearly established with the forces of heaven behind it."

Nancy shook on the floor and clutched Robin's hand as the vision faded. Nancy was literally on the same battleground she had perceived in the spirit for years. Her perceptions turned into revelation of the intense spiritual warfare in which the group was constantly engaged. This time, Jesus had met her in the combat zone and removed the daggers inflicted both spiritually and physically. It was a life-changing encounter with her King.

It's Only A Shadow

EPILOGUE

It's Only a Shadow presents stories from "outside the cave" to challenge the prevailing mindset that does not acknowledge the existence of spiritual warfare. It is a wakeup call to believers in Jesus Christ who have been lulled into apathy or even denial concerning spiritual realities in daily life. These accounts from three different voices are meant to provoke questions concerning the supernatural realm and encourage exploration of God's word on the matter.

There are more stories to tell concerning real battles with powers that lurk in the shadows, some of which will appear in the sequel, *Prophetic Warrior*. However, before these stories can be heard, one must first recognize the existence of the realm of the spirit and then seek to understand the subtle ways in which he or she is already participating with that realm.

It is imperative to me to present these stories to counterbalance the current deluge of media that portrays the supernatural realm through a single, "harmless entertainment" lens. Sorcery, nephilim, vampires, and many other ungodly things dominate this lens. Masses of people become fans and followers of these stories, eagerly awaiting the next installment. Relating to and imagining with the prevalent themes in this media through reading a book or watching a movie translates into agreement with and acceptance of the underlying philosophies. Both adults and children are lulled into unwittingly receiving from the sources of power portrayed because approval is the default when one participates. It is anything but harmless.

Brandy shares her heart for the book as well:

> "Individuals in this story are simple, real-life folks, who have a calling and destiny. *It's Only a Shadow* chronicles their testimonies. God may use men, women, and children to

Epilogue

bring His kingdom, but it is Christ within each believer that brings the victory. No man can take any glory or credit for God's actions of love, yet we are the vessels of honor that he chooses to use to bring forth His will on earth. We have been given dominion, authority, and power to release the Blessing, God's goodness, and glory, upon all of mankind (Genesis 1:26-28).

When light and darkness face off, there is a great explosion, and intense battles occur in the heavens and on earth with the angelic and demonic forces. When light invades the darkness, there can be great wrath and retaliation from the enemy. These battles are real and can be 'hard to believe' with our natural minds. Jesus spoke of this in John 3, where He explained the kingdom of heaven to Nicodemus, a religious leader of his day. Nicodemus did not understand because he was reasoning with his mind as to how he could actually be born again in his mother's womb. Jesus was speaking of the spirit and being born of the spirit, yet in his mind, Nicodemus could not comprehend such perceptions. Jesus said,

> 'If I have told you earthly things and you do not believe, how will you believe if I tell you heavenly things' (John 3:12 NKJV).

Jesus went on to say in John 5:19 (NKJV),

> 'Most assuredly, I say to you, the son can do nothing of Himself, but what He sees the Father do; for whatever He does, the son also does in like manner.'

Paul prayed in Ephesians 1:17,18 (NKJV) we would be given wisdom and revelation in the knowledge of Him, and that the eyes of our understanding would be opened.

As we record these events, we write of the reality of supernatural occurrences. In our culture, so much is not believed unless you can 'see it,' 'prove it,' or have encountered it

Epilogue

for yourself (John 20:24-29). When I first told of the supernatural occurrences, they were hard to believe, and then many could not or would not believe what I shared. How wonderful it was when the Lord put this team of believers in my life who had been given understanding and faith to believe what the word of God says. They understood the reality of the 'unseen world' (II Corinthians 4:18) and a supernatural life manifested in people.

As we recall our encounters, visions, and real life circumstances and share them, it comes alive as a movie on a screen. I've always wanted to see books or movies that reveal God's army, angels, church, and power as a reality. The only heroes in this book are God the Father, Jesus the Son, and Holy Spirit! All honor and praise go to HIM, our eternal God!"

It's Only a Shadow describes spiritual battles, real wounds, and high stakes, but the good news is we are not defenseless in spiritual warfare. On the contrary, we have access to decisive, victorious power through our covenant with Jesus Christ. I started my journey of discovering spiritual warfare by reading the book, *Shadow Boxing*, by Henry Malone. A fellow warrior and colleague, Lauren Caldwell, has written two books that explain the same content to kids. I highly recommend these books to adults as well: *There's No Junior Holy Spirit: A Supernatural Training Manual for Youth (Tales from the Throne)*, and *The Gospel of the Kingdom for Kids, Tweens, and Teens (Tales from the Throne)*.

Brandy and the team she assembled have a website with rich resources for training warriors, freeing captives, and building the Kingdom at http://thegardenstc.org.

Reading the books about spiritual warfare is a step to opening up the mind to the possibility that there is a very real spiritual realm that exists in tan-

Epilogue

dem with the natural world we experience with our senses. However, according to 1 Corinthians 2:14 (NKJV),

> "But the natural man does not receive the things of the Spirit of God, for they are foolishness to him; nor can he know them, because they are spiritually discerned."

Therefore spiritual things are best discerned by the spirit. It can be a really simple decision that one can make to willfully command the mind, will, and emotions to submit to the spirit that is inside and to receive revelation of spiritual realities. I call that "flesh down, spirit up and in charge." I don't have to feel anything; I just have to believe that it is true. In that posture, the spirit man that I have inside, who is already operating in the spiritual realm, can receive true revelation of the spiritual dimension.

Those of us who have accepted Jesus as our Savior and have received the Holy Spirit are all equipped with fully functioning, reborn spirits who can be accurately trained by the best teacher, Holy

Spirit. Jesus describes Holy Spirit as the spirit of truth in John 14:16-18,

> "And I will ask the Father, and he will give you another Counselor to be with you forever— the Spirit of truth. The world cannot accept him, because it neither sees him nor knows him. But you know him, for he lives with you and will be in you."

Who better to train us than the actual spirit of truth? Jesus tells us that Holy Spirit will teach us all things in John 14:26,

> "But the Counselor, the Holy Spirit, whom the Father will send in my name, will teach you all things and will remind you of everything I have said to you."

Therefore the decision is a simple choice we as Christians can make with our wills to allow Holy Spirit to teach our spirits about the unseen realm with which our spirits are already interacting. The key point is realizing that there is spiritual dimension and actively choosing to be open to learning about it.

In her song, "Only a Shadow", Misty Edwards poses the questions: "Is not life more than meets the eye? Is there not more to life than what we see? Is there not more to life than what meets the eye? Is what we see only a shadow?"

If your answer is yes to any of these questions, you may be recognizing that eternal life starts **now**. Jesus came to save us from our sin, not our circumstances. He equipped us to wage war on the forces of evil, and the battle has already begun. Don't wait until death places you in the middle of a spiritual existence. Allow Holy Spirit to teach you the ways of the Kingdom of Heaven, now. If you do not have a relationship with Jesus, you might consider making Him not only your savior, but your lord and master as well, so you will have His resources with which to fight.

The distinction between **savior** and **lord** is noted in Acts 2:36,

"Therefore let all Israel be assured of this: God

has made this Jesus, whom you crucified, both Lord and Christ."

In the original language of the bible, Christ meant the anointed one who was appointed by God to carry out a specific function which was to shed His blood to **save** you from your sins - savior. However, Lord, meant **master** or **supreme authority**. This verse attributes both titles to Jesus, and the distinction becomes important in spiritual warfare.

The declaration that Jesus is not only savior but lord and master in your life makes it clear to the demons opposing you which side you have chosen and what authority backs you up when you war in the name of Jesus. This pronouncement is often overlooked but needs to be clearly stated.

The time has come for you to allow Jesus to open your spiritual understanding. Only then will you be able to take your place among the ranks of His army. The things that have hindered you are mere shadows. Jesus and the splendor of His glory – that is reality.

APPENDIX

Prayer for Salvation

If you have not made Jesus Christ your personal Lord and Savior, and you desire this with all your heart, then please, join me in prayer:

"Heavenly Father, I choose to believe with all my heart that you love me. I believe that Jesus Christ is Your Son, the Son of God, and that He is God in the flesh. I believe that You sent Him to this earth to save me. Thank you. I believe He died on the cross for my sins, and He was dead and buried three days and then rose again from the dead and that He ascended to heaven and is now seated at Your right hand and is returning again.

Father, please forgive me for all my sin and iniquity, and I choose to forgive others who have sinned against me. I give you all my heart and choose to live with you forever. I believe I have been born again according to Your word, and that I have been transferred out of the kingdom of darkness and into the kingdom of light.

Now, I ask for Holy Spirit to fill me. Jesus, baptize me in Holy Spirit and fullness. Thank you, Lord, for loving me. Amen."

Below are the scriptural references for the previous prayer:

John 14:6 – "Jesus answered, 'I am the way and the truth and the life. No one comes to the Father except through me.'"

Romans 10:7-13 – "or 'Who will descend into the deep?' (that is, to bring Christ up from the dead). But what does it say? 'The word is near you; it is in your mouth and in your heart,' that is, the word of faith we are proclaiming: That if you confess with your mouth, 'Jesus is Lord,' and believe in your heart that God raised him from the dead, you will be saved. For it is with your heart that you believe and are justified, and it is with your mouth that you confess and are saved. As the Scripture says, 'Anyone who trusts in him will never be put to shame.' For there is no difference between Jew and Gentile — the same Lord is Lord of all and richly blesses all who call on him, for, 'Everyone who calls on the name of the Lord will be saved.'"

John 3:16-18 – "For God so loved the world that he gave his one and only Son, that whoever believes in him shall not perish but have eternal life. For God did not send his Son into the world to condemn the world, but to save the world through him. Whoever believes in him is not condemned, but whoever does not believe stands condemned already because he has not believed in the name of God's one and only Son."

II Corinthians 5:17 – "Therefore, if anyone is in Christ, he is a new creation; the old has gone, the new has come!"

John 3:3-7 –"In reply Jesus declared, 'I tell you the truth, no one can see the kingdom of God unless he is born again.' 'How can a man be born when he is old?' Nicodemus asked. 'Surely he cannot enter a second time into his mother's womb to be born!' Jesus answered, 'I tell you the truth, no one can enter the kingdom of God unless he is born of water and the Spirit. Flesh gives birth to flesh, but the Spirit gives birth to spirit. You should not be surprised at my saying, 'You must be born again.'"

I Corinthians 15:3-5 – "For what I received I passed on to you as of first importance: that Christ died for our sins according to the Scriptures, that he was buried, that he was raised on the third day according to the Scriptures, and that he appeared to Peter, and then to the Twelve."

II Corinthians 5:21– "God made him who had no sin to be sin for us, so that in him we might become the righteousness of God."

Colossians 1:13 – "For he has rescued us from the dominion of darkness and brought us into the kingdom of the Son he loves."

Luke 11:9-13 – "So I say to you: Ask and it will be given to you; seek and you will find; knock and the door will be opened to you. For everyone who asks receives; he who seeks finds; and to him who knocks, the door will be opened. Which of you fathers, if your son asks for a fish, will give him a snake instead? Or if he asks for an egg, will give him a scorpion? If you then, though you are evil, know how to give good gifts to your children, how much more will your Father in heaven give the Holy Spirit to those who ask him!"

Acts 1:8 – "But you will receive power when the Holy Spirit comes on you; and you will be my witnesses in Jerusalem, and in all Judea and Samaria, and to the ends of the earth."

I Timothy 3:16 – "Beyond all question, the mystery of godliness is great:
He appeared in a body,
was vindicated by the Spirit,
was seen by angels,
was preached among the nations,
was believed on in the world,
was taken up in glory."

Declaration to make Jesus Lord and Master

If you want to make Jesus your Lord and Master, join me in declaring:

"Jesus Christ is my only Lord and Master. According to Acts 2:36, Jesus is both Lord and Christ. He is God. He is the Son of God. He is the King of Kings and Lord of Lords. He was crucified for the sins of the world and was dead, buried, descended into hell, resurrected three days later, and now sits at the right hand of God the Father."

Prayers for MORE

If you have been born again and filled with Holy Spirit and you desire MORE and want to encounter the Lord's presence afresh and anew, join me in these prayers:

"Father, in the name of Jesus I thank you for loving me, and I ask according to Ephesians 1:17-19, that you would give me the spirit of wisdom and revelation in the knowledge of Him, Jesus, and the eyes of my understanding would be enlightened; that I may know what is the hope of His calling and what are the riches of the glory of His inheritance in the saints, and what is the exceeding greatness of His power toward us who believe, according to the working of His mighty power which He worked in Christ when He raised Him from the dead and seated Him at His right hand in the heavenly places. Amen."

"Father, according to Colossians 3:9-12, I ask in Jesus name, that I would be filled with the knowledge of His will in all wisdom and spiritual understanding; that I would walk worthy of the Lord, fully pleasing Him, being fruitful in every good work and increasing in the knowledge of God; strengthened with all might, according to His glorious power. Amen."

www.ingramcontent.com/pod-product-compliance
Lightning Source LLC
Chambersburg PA
CBHW050632300426
44112CB00012B/1766